Purpose-driven Organizations

"Many companies have a statement of purpose. Not many have it specified in terms of knowledge, motivation and action. There are less that integrate it in their strategy. And very few harmonize it with the purposes of their people. This book explains how to do all these things."
—Antonio Argandoña, *Emeritus Professor, IESE Business School, Spain*

"Establishing a good purpose for the organization, with business sense and consistent with the common good of the society, is primordial for a conscious management. This book will help to reflect on corporate purpose, in its institutional role and as a driver for management and for sound leadership."
—Domènec Melé, *Holder of the Chair of Business Ethics, IESE Business School, Spain*

"Purpose has become a popular term in the field of business management. However, few can unambiguously articulate its multi-faceted conceptual meaning. Even less know how to turn purpose into concrete action in organizations. The book of Rey, Bastons, and Sotok fulfills such needs with clarity, depth, and elegance."
—Yih-teen Lee, *Professor, Department of Managing People in Organizations, IESE Business School, Spain*

"Purpose is of central importance both to individuals, and to organizations. A book devoted to the exploration of these issues is most welcome, and could benefit anyone interested in helping to form a more purpose-driven organization."
—Tyler J. VanderWeele, *Harvard T.H. Chan School of Public Health, USA*

"Corporate purpose is a popular topic; one that unfortunately is not always truly understood. This book's authors not only understand the true, core definition of an organization's purpose—"the very broad reason for its existence"—but also provide an insightful analysis of how to make it real in the enterprise."
—Roger Bolton, *President of the Arthur W. Page Society, USA*

"This book provides thoughtful direction for the new organization and the people in it. The authors' categories of purpose describe a way for managers to develop structures for living up to common economic goals without losing a sense of discipline and humanity."
—Laura Nash, *Cambridge, MA, USA*

"We are navigating in a new economic and social cycle which experts refer to as the purpose economy. Those organizations with a clear and relevant purpose perform better than competitors. This book helps you to understand the strategic importance of having and activating the corporate character, and makes you to realise the role that companies can play in society."

—José Manuel Velasco, *Past President of the Global Alliance for Public Relations and Communication Management, Spain*

Carlos Rey • Miquel Bastons • Phil Sotok
Editors

Purpose-driven Organizations

Management Ideas for a Better World

palgrave
macmillan

Editors
Carlos Rey
Chair Management by Missions and Corporate
Governance
Universitat Internacional de Catalunya
Barcelona, Spain

Miquel Bastons
School of Economics and Social Sciences
Universitat Internacional de Catalunya
Barcelona, Spain

Phil Sotok
DPMC
Barcelona, Spain

CORPORATE EXCELLENCE

CENTRE FOR REPUTATION LEADERSHIP

uLc
barcelona
Chair in Management
by Missions and
Corporate Governance

DPMC

ISBN 978-3-030-17673-0   ISBN 978-3-030-17674-7   (eBook)
https://doi.org/10.1007/978-3-030-17674-7

Foreword

In my early twenties, I almost quit my first significant leadership role. I had been elected executive director of a new non-profit which at its seasonal peak involved hundreds of adult volunteers. Most of the year-round the staff were almost twice my age. The pressure felt immense. But I was elected because ostensibly, without kids yet, I had more free time. There was really no one else who wanted the position.

In a moment of decision, I thought about just being a vessel for the organization's purpose and doing my best. I remember falling short of this ideal at times but it was enough of a shift to go on.

I was reminded of this story when I read the book you're holding, *The Purpose-Driven Organization*.

It's rare that I finish a business book because few say things that are new. But this book has a timeless, incontrovertible idea that sadly feels radical today——the most effective organizations have individuals who are deeply aligned with their own purpose and the alignment of this purpose with that of an organization is possible. And the reason this is possible is because ultimate meaning, a telos, is accessible even to the largest enterprises if one's eyes are lifted upwards. While maybe uncommon, this idea is not entirely novel. In 1958, Dave Packard said something similar, "As we look to [sic] future we must keep opportunity for each individual to have opportunity to achieve his aspirations—to utilize his abilities for common benefit of us all. Our underlying objectives [sic] to find the best balance between the individual responsibility and ... to combine with it a desire and incentive to join this in an objective to contribute to the strength of the corporation as a whole."[1]

What follows is an entry in my journal, handwritten but transcribed here, where I was ruminating on the nature of humanization and purpose in large organizations. I shared it privately with a friend who turned out to be one of the co-authors of the Purpose-Driven Organization. I was asked if this entry could be used for an introduction. I was hesitant at first but then I read a draft of this book and met one of the editors, Dr. Carlos Rey. The book responds to the questions in my entry. Dr. Rey's own testimony closes this book, but really it should have been the introduction. I suggest perhaps reading it first as it lends life and vigor to the work of the rest of his colleagues.

From a Journal Entry Dated November 24, 2018

What is it that contributes to the banality of many jobs? A disconnection between one's efforts and the manifestation of that effort. That manifestation is often best received physically. There is something satisfying say about farming in a way that is not evident in much knowledge work.

Focus also has something to do with it. A diffusion of effort seems to rob one of the opportunity to realize some weight behind one's contributions.

So many of the essentials of modern living are enabled by products of industrial scale organizations and processes. But these organizations and processes seem to tend towards dehumanization. Novelty, autonomy, connection seem to be missing, almost antithetical to the needs of the industrial ethos. Does it have to be this way? Do large scale enterprises require de-individuation? Is this level of de-individuation an artifact of the current state of technology and what it takes to marshal human capital towards large scale and repeatable ends? Will this diminish as technologies such as robotics and AI supplant much of human labor? We don't lament over the banality of gears in a motor.

What would a large scale (10's of thousands) enterprise that fully realizes humanity look like? Would it be more like a city, where each individual is pursuing individual ends in a cooperative state? Is it like open source software? Where self-motivated individuals create and refine a product driven by commonly understood ethos? Wikipedia?

What is the dehumanization being referenced? Tedious, pointless tasks. Fear leading to hierarchical obsequiousness. A disconnection to purpose.

What can be lost however is that the world's advancement relies on scaled organizations. Dams. Medical equipment. Schools. National security. These all can't and shouldn't be vacated. But how much humanization is attainable in these institutional efforts? And what is one's role in these institutions? It's a question of one's obligation to the causes as well as thinking fundamentally about the telos of large scale organizations.

Maybe the current limits of how humanized a large organization can be is a reflection of the limits of human societies in general.

And one does their best in their circle of influence.

Hewlett-Packard   Louis Kim
San Diego, CA, USA

Note

1. https://historycenter.agilent.com/category/packard-speeches/page/2.

Acknowledgments

We want to express our gratitude to the contributors who have co-authored the different chapters of this book. We thank them for their generosity and dedication not only in writing their specific chapters but also in acting as reviewers of other chapters. They made it possible for the book to be built on solid academic research and, at the same time, be written in a way that is easily accessible to managers.

Alongside, we thank the army of practitioners and scholars—including the blind reviewers—who offered their insights, examples, and criticism, all of which enhanced and made this book more relevant for today's business person:

Alberto Ribera
Alfonso Aguiló
Antonio Argandoña
Antonio Hidalgo
Ayse Yemiscigil
Bryan Lanser
Domènec Mele
Eduard Fitó
Eudald Parera
Fátima Delgado
Fernando Cerdeña
Florent Amion
France Allen
Gabriel Monllau
Gonzalo Orejas
Imad Younis
Inés Rey

Jaime Gonzalez Baizán
Jeff Disher
Jerry Zandstra
Jianbo Niu
Joan Fontrodona
Jon Lanning
José Antonio Fonseca Pires
Jose Fonseca
Jose Porfirio
Kay McCarthy
Juan de Dios López Uceda
Laura Nash
Manuel Guillén-Parra
Manuel Jiménez Maña
Mark Bryme
Markus Groeber
Mary Chiasson
Matt Potts
Mayte Marquez
Michael Hoffman
Miguel Ángel Ariño
Mike Lanser
Peter Lubin
Ramon Casadesuss
Ramón Pes
Ricard Casas
Robert McNulty
Ronan O'Farrell
Rudi Loossens
Sarah Mecredy
Tomás Baviera
Vicente Blanes
Yih-teen Lee

Contents

Part I   Understanding Purpose-driven Organizations   1

1   **The New Logic of Purpose Within the Organization**   3
    Carlos Rey, Jon San Cristobal Velasco, and Juan Almandoz

2   **Harmonization of Personal and Organizational Purpose**   17
    Carlos Rey and Ivan Malbašić

3   **Three Dimensions of Purpose: Knowledge, Motivation, and
    Action**   29
    Carlos Rey and Miquel Bastons

4   **Why Purpose Needs Strategy (and Vice Versa)**   43
    Carlos Rey and Joan E. Ricart

5   **Purpose-driven Leadership**   57
    Pablo Cardona, Carlos Rey, and Nick Craig

Part II   Creating Purpose-driven Organizations   73

6   **Agile Purpose: Overcoming Bureaucracy**   75
    Carlos Rey, Nuno Pitta, Donatas Ramonas, and Phil Sotok

7   **Key Factors in Purpose Internalization**   87
    Carlos Rey, Frederic Marimon, and Marta Mas-Machuca

8   **Nurturing Personal Purpose at Work**   97
    Carlos Rey, Juan Almandoz, and Alex Montaner

9   **(Re)Discovering Organizational Purpose**   107
    Clara Fontán, Ángel Alloza, and Carlos Rey

10 **Measuring the Purpose Strength**   119
    Alvaro Lleo, Carlos Rey, and Nuria Chinchilla

Epilogue   131

Index   135

Notes on Contributors

Ángel Alloza is CEO of Corporate Excellence—Centre for Reputation Leadership. Prior to this position, he worked at J. Walter Thompson, and at Millward Brown International in Spain and Portugal. Later, he joined BBVA, where he served as the Director of Strategy and Evaluation for the global BBVA Group Communications and Brand area. He has written numerous articles in reference publications and is co-author of *Atrapados por el consumo* and *Corporate Reputation*. Alloza is also an academic research delegate of the Global Alliance for Public Relations and Communication Management and a member of the Arthur W. Page Society. In addition, he is co-director and professor of The Global Chief Communication Officer Executive Program at ESADE, honorary professor at the University of Malaga and academic assistant at internationally renowned business schools such as ESADE, IE Business School and IESE, and universities such as Complutense University of Madrid, Universitat Autònoma de Barcelona, Jaume I, Ramón Llull, Carlos III and Universidad Pontificia de Salamanca. He holds a BA degree in Psychology from the Complutense University of Madrid, a PCD title from IESE, and a PhD from Jaume I University.

Juan Almandoz is an Associate Professor in the Department of Managing People in Organizations at IESE Business School. His background includes experience in actuarial consulting, corporate banking, and the management of non-profit organizations. He holds a joint PhD in Organizational Behavior and a master's degree in Sociology from Harvard Business School and an MBA from the Cox School of Business. His work has been published in prestigious journals such as the *Academy of Management Journal* and *Administrative Science Quarterly*. He participates in research in leadership, organizations with dual missions, institutional theory, and top management teams and boards of directors. His dissertation focused on the strategic and entrepreneurial implications of community and financial missions in the founding teams of local banks.

Miquel Bastons is an Associate Professor of Organizational Behavior and Ethics in the School of Economics and Social Sciences at the International University of Catalonia, Spain. He holds a PhD in Philosophy and a PhD in Management. His research focuses on organizational decision-making and business ethics. His work has been published in the *Journal of Business Ethics*, *Journal of Management & Organization*, *Journal of Agricultural and Environmental Ethics*, *Science and Engineering Ethics* and *Long Range Planning*. He has been a section editor of the *Handbook of Virtue Ethics in Business and Management* and is a reviewer for the *Journal of Business Ethics*, *Journal of Management & Organization*, *Journal of Academic Ethics*, *Journal of Agricultural and Environmental Ethics* and *European Management Journal*.

Pablo Cardona is Dean of the School of Management and Communication at UNIR (Universidad Internacional de La Rioja, Spain). Previously, he has been a professor at CEIBS (Shanghai) and IESE (Barcelona). His interests lie in the areas of leadership, organizational behavior, and cross-cultural research. His work has been published in leading management journals, including the *Strategic Management Journal*, and *Group & Organization Management*. He has received three awards from the Academy of Management and has written several practitioner books on leadership and management such as *How to Develop Leadership Competencies*, *Growing as a Leader*, and *Management by Missions*.

Nuria Chinchilla is a Professor in the Department of Managing People in Organizations, Head of the Chair "Carmina Roca & Rafael Pich-Aguilera" of Women in Leadership, and founder of the International Center on Work and Family at IESE Business School. She is also a frequent guest speaker at European, American, and African Universities, and at international conferences, as well as a visiting professor at business schools such as IPADE in Mexico, ISE in Brazil, INALDE in Colombia, IDE in Ecuador, PAD in Peru, ESE in Chile, IAE in Argentina, IEEM in Uruguay, Lagos Business School in Nigeria and Strathmore University in Kenya. Chinchilla was named "Best Manager of the Year" by the Spanish Federation of Executive Women (FEDEPE). She is also co-author of several books, such as *Masters of Our Destiny: How to Balance Professional, Family and Personal Life* (2007), *Being a*

Family-Responsible Company: Luxury or Need? (2006), *Female Ambition: How to Reconcile Work and Family* (Palgrave Macmillan 2005). She is the only woman on Spain's "Top Ten Management" listing (www.toptenms.com).

Nick Craig is the author of the newly published book, *Leading from Purpose*, and President of the Core Leadership Institute, where he guides executives on the journey to discover and lead with purpose. In 2007, Craig began collaborating with Bill George at Harvard Business School; this led them to co-authoring, *Finding Your True North: A Personal Guide*, which became the course book for the Harvard Business School MBA class on Authentic Leadership Development (ALD). Craig is also the co-author with Scott Snook of the 2014 *Harvard Business Review* article "From Purpose to Impact" and *The Discover Your True North Fieldbook*. He has worked with organizations that include Ben & Jerry's, Heineken, ING Bank, LEGO®, Unilever, and the United States Military Academy at West Point.

Clara Fontán is the Intelligence and Knowledge Senior Manager at Corporate Excellence—Centre for Reputation Leadership and an associate professor at Universidad Loyola Andalucía, Spain. She holds a bachelor's degree in Communication from the University of Seville, Spain; a master's degree in Corporate and Political Communication from the University of Navarra, Spain, and George Washington University, USA, and a PhD from the UCM. She has had extensive international training on intangible assets management, which includes the Global Chief Communication Program from ESADE Business School, a certificate on corporate reputation management from Reputation Institute, a certificate from the Corporate Reputation Centre at the University of Oxford, and the Executive Program on Intangible Assets Management for the Brand and the Reputation from EOI.

Álvaro Lleó is an Associate Professor at the Industrial Management Department at Tecnun School of Engineering, University of Navarra. He holds his PhD from the Polytechnic University of Valencia, where he also studied Industrial Engineering and Industrial Management. He was a research fellow at Harvard University and a visiting scholar at Bentley University. Previously, he has worked on a different project in the automobile sector, and also as a human resources consultant. He has supervised 2 doctoral theses and has participated in 12 research projects. He has more than 35 publications in academic Journals and at international conferences. He is also a reviewer of articles for journals such as *Personnel Review* and *Business Ethics: A European Review*. He is the academic director of the project Measuring the Purpose Strength.

Ivan Malbašić is an Assistant Professor with the Faculty of Organization and Informatics at the University of Zagreb, Croatia. He holds his PhD degree from the University of Maribor, Slovenia. He teaches courses at the undergraduate and graduate levels in organization, management, and organizational behavior. His main research and publications concern the role of organizational values in business, organizational behavior, public management, and organizational effectiveness in general. His work has been published in several leading business and management journals, including the *Journal of Business Ethics*, *Management Decision*, and *Journal of Human Values*.

Frederic Marimon is a Tenured Professor at the Universitat Internacional de Catalunya (UIC Barcelona). He holds a PhD in Business Administration and has a degree in Industrial Engineering from Polytechnic University of Catalonia in Barcelona, and a master's in Business and Administration from IESE in Barcelona. His focus is on operations management, mainly in the areas of quality, e-quality measurement, and in services companies. His articles have been published in international academic journals, most of which are in the quality management area, and also some papers that analyze the diffusion phenomenon of management standards (i.e. ISO 9000, ISO 14000, etc.).

Marta Mas-Machuca holds a PhD in Business Administration from the Universitat Politècnica de Catalunya (UPC) in Spain. She was a manager of a business unit for the Altran Group, a consulting company, for 6 years. Since 2013, she has worked as a lecturer in the Department of Economy and Business Organization at the International University of Catalonia in Spain, teaching strategic management and human resources. She collaborates on research with the Chair in Mission Leadership and Corporate Governance. She has participated in several research projects, and she is the author of several books, articles and working papers.

Alex Montaner is an executive coach and expert in leadership. He works as a consultant at DPMC, training teams to develop a more agile and meaningful culture. He conducts Personal Purpose workshops and coaches top managers on that path, and is a member of the IESE Executive Coaching Team. He covers a broad spectrum of sectors, both at the national and international levels. He was a Business Unit Director at Procter & Gamble. He has a master's in Business Administration from ESADE and has attended the Management Development Program (PDD) from IESE. He is a ACC-ICF certified coach in Co-Active Coaching by the Coaches Training Institute

(CTI). He holds a Master in Neuro Linguistic Programming and Trainer NLP by the Gestalt Institute.

Nuno Pitta holds a BS degree in Economics and Mathematics from ISEG—Lisbon, and a Management Development Program (PDG) from IESE. Since 2013, he has been the CEO of DPMC, providing strategy and change management consulting in the development of organizational purpose and mission-driven management. Previously he was a corporate governance consultant at PwC for 6 years, working directly with clients such as Novartis, Camper, Chevron Texaco, Sara Lee, Sony, Indukern Group, Ferrer and others. He was CEO of the Dows Group (an electronics retailing chain), and has held various management roles in different countries (Portugal, Angola and Spain).

Donatas Ramonas has more than 16 years of experience in training and consulting. He studied and participated in various internship programs at Princeton, Chicago, London, Stockholm and Oslo universities and training companies. He has also been the head of the Project Management program at the ISM University of Management and Economics, Executive School. He is a managing partner of the management consulting company CRC Consulting in Vilnius, Lithuania, and serves on Board of Director committees for profit and non-profit organizations.

Carlos Rey is a Professor of Strategic Management and Director of the Chair Management by Missions and Corporate Governance at Universitat Internacional de Catalunya (UIC Barcelona) and the Founder of DPMC. During the past 15 years, he has collaborated as a consultant and researcher in the development of organizational purpose with companies such as Coca-Cola, Sony, Repsol, ISS Facility Services, Bristol Myers Squib, and 100s more. He received the extraordinary doctorate award for his PhD dissertation on organizational mission and purpose. He is co-author of *Management by Missions*, published in six languages, and has written other books as well as articles published in leading journals like *Long Range Planning* and *Journal of Business Ethics*.

Joan E. Ricart is Carl Schrøder Professor of Strategic Management at IESE Business School. He has been Chairman of the Strategic Management Department at the IESE Business School for the past 23 years. He is a Fellow of the SMS and EURAM, and was the Founding president of the European Academy of Management (EURAM) and President of the Strategic Management Society (SMS). He has authored several books and articles in leading journals such as the *Strategic Management Journal, Harvard Business Review, Journal of International Business Studies,* and *Econometrica* or the *Quarterly Journal of Economics.*

Phil Sotok is Founder of VentureSource Corporation, a global supplier of engineered products to the automotive industry, with offices in the US, China, Spain, and Mexico. In 2017, Phil launched DPMC North America, a management consultancy specializing in mission-driven management and virtuous leadership. Prior to these endeavors, he worked in various engineering, finance and international business development roles for Chrysler, Magna, and Johnson Controls Corporation. He has a BS degree in Economics and Mathematics from Hope College and an MBA from Thunderbird School of Global Management. In addition to providing leadership to VentureSource and DPMC, Sotok is an investor and advisor in two start-ups. One is an e-learning platform in West Michigan and the other, a social enterprise in Guatemala City.

Jon San Cristobal Velasco is the Managing Director of Huf Portuguesa since 1991. He was Country Manager of Ficosa International Portugal and Manager of Fico-Cables, Lda (1997–2007). He is a member of the Advisory Board of the Center Business Council (CEC), the General Council of Business School, AESE, and the Chair in Management by Missions and Corporate Governance, Universitat Internacional de Catalunya (UIC Barcelona). He has worked in the Portuguese industry and has been living in Portugal since 1982. He holds a degree in Law from the University of the Basque Country. He had attended the Senior Management Program, AESE Business School (2000) and was a member of the Board of Directors of the Business Association of Viseu Region (AIRV) 1995–1998.

List of Figures

Fig. 1.1   Symbolic representation of unity   11
Fig. 2.1   Purpose fluidity   21
Fig. 2.2   Purpose synergy   23
Fig. 3.1   3D model of purpose (Based on Rey, C., & Bastons, M. (2018). Three dimensions of effective mission implementation. *Long Range Planning, 51*, 580–585)   33
Fig. 3.2   Linear and oblique approach for purpose development   37
Fig. 4.1   Illustration of a "purpose model canvas"   52
Fig. 6.1   Interplay between unity and alignment   79
Fig. 6.2   Illustration of an agile purpose chart   82
Fig. 8.1   Holistic conceptualization of purpose (Source: Adapted from Rey, C., & Bastons, M. (2018). Three dimensions of effective mission implementation. *Long Range Planning, 51*(4), 580–585. / Graphic Design: Reproduced with permission from Freeland Communication Studio SL)   100
Fig. 8.2   Fit between the three dimensions of purpose (Graphic Design: Reproduced with permission from Freeland Communication Studio SL)   101
Fig. 8.3   Fundamental undertakings of purpose development (Graphic Design: Reproduced with permission from Freeland Communication Studio SL)   102
Fig. 9.1   A roadmap for (re)discovering corporate purpose   109
Fig. 9.2   Purpose as the intersection of three dimensions of 'being'   112
Fig. 10.1   The Purpose Strength Model   120
Fig. 10.2   Shared purpose and its dimensions   121
Fig. 10.3   Individual outcomes of having a shared purpose   123

Fig. 10.4   Collective outcomes of having a shared response   124
Fig. 10.5   Organizational drivers that precede the shared purpose generation   125
Fig. 10.6   Accelerators (or decelerators) of shared purpose generation   127

List of Tables

Table 1.1   Fundamental traits of the new logic of purpose   6
Table 2.1   Harmonizing purpose in organizations   20
Table 3.1   Examples of 'linear' frameworks for purpose development   31
Table 4.1   Analytical, business model, and institutional perspectives   44
Table 4.2   The three strategic perspectives integrated with purpose   50
Table 5.1   Fundamentals of purpose-driven leadership (PDL)   63
Table 6.1   Basic management tools   77
Table 7.1   Significance of the seven dimensions of purpose internalization   88

Part I

Understanding Purpose-driven Organizations

1

The New Logic of Purpose Within the Organization

Carlos Rey, Jon San Cristobal Velasco,
and Juan Almandoz

> *During a full day of onboard training for new employees, the CEO was asked to explain, firsthand, the purpose of the company. When he ended his talk, a young man raised his hand and said: "I love that I work for a company with a real purpose but, tell me one thing … what should **my** purpose be in this company?" The CEO was a bit surprised and visibly unsure on how to answer the question. The instructor of the training—a very wise man—took the floor and said: "Today the CEO has explained to you the company's purpose, but for **your** purpose in this company …, that's something you will need to discover for yourself."*

As organizations search for a more humanistic approach to management, there is an increasing call to embrace "an intentional and broader focus on purpose."[1] The idea of purpose has been around management for decades. In

C. Rey (✉)
Universitat Internacional de Catalunya,
Barcelona, Spain
e-mail: carlosrey@uic.es

J. S. C. Velasco
Huf Portuguesa, Tondela, Portugal
e-mail: Jon.Velasco@huf-group.com

J. Almandoz
Department of Managing People in Organizations, IESE Business School,
Barcelona, Spain
e-mail: JAlmandoz@iese.edu

© The Author(s) 2019
C. Rey et al. (eds.), *Purpose-driven Organizations*,
https://doi.org/10.1007/978-3-030-17674-7_1

fact, organizations that have formally stated their organizational purpose are now quite common. However, the presence of purpose is not a phenomenon exclusive to the organization alone. Evidence from the field shows that the idea of purpose is also present and it develops at an individual level within the organizations.[2]

In this introductory chapter, we argue that the fulfillment of personal purpose *within organizational purpose* is the essence of truly purpose-driven organizations. But discovering this scope requires one to evolve from a neoclassical logic of management to one that is based on, what we will call here, the new *management logic of purpose.*

Recognizing Purpose

Whether collective or individual, purpose represents the "why" of our actions and efforts. And, more importantly, it specifies our contribution to this world and to the society in which we live. The presence of purpose is a trend that has been growing in recent decades[3] and, we believe, will certainly continue to grow in the future. Most notably because the concept of purpose is becoming a necessary and key element for creating meaningful organizations in a competitive environment that is strongly marked by inconsistency and uncertainty.

At the organizational level, purpose is generally associated with concepts such as mission, vision, or ultimate aspirations. However, purpose is commonly considered as the basic idea—the essence—that underlies and sustains the meaning of these concepts. More specifically, purpose can be considered as the foundation of the mission.[4] Think for example on Tata's purpose: "to improve the quality of life for the communities we serve."[5] In this sense, purpose is not a mere declaration to stakeholders, but is, in fact, the very broad reason for its existence.[6] Purpose represents an overarching commitment to society that includes broader aims, such as "making a difference," or "improving lives," or "reducing harm" and "[Purpose] acknowledges the interdependence of business and society— [as] one cannot flourish without the other."[7]

Purpose is usually defined in short sentences or ideas that express the positive impact and legacy a company aims to leave on this world. Purpose is inspiring, helping companies go beyond their self-imposed limitations and strive for the seemingly impossible. For example, the purpose of Disney is "to use our imagination to bring happiness to millions." 3 M hopes to "improve every company, every home, every life." Google is "to organize the world's information and make it universally accessible and useful." Purpose can also be found by looking at areas where people feel excluded, or where their potential to contribute has been disregarded or overlooked by society.[8] This is the case, for example of La Fageda, a Catalonian yogurt manufacturer where almost all its workers have a mental disability. Their purpose is to "make work meaningful."

And we know, when companies are true to their purpose, ordinary employees can do extraordinary things. Consider, for example, the behavior of staff members at the Taj Mahal Palace, Mumbai, a hotel of the Tata Group. On November 26, 2008, ten armed terrorists seized the hotel. Without hesitation, staff members, in the middle of what was described as a war-like situation, formed a human chain helping guests to escape by shielding them from terrorists' bullets. No one ordered this, there were no manuals or instructions on how to act in such an extreme situation. Some of the staff were wounded and others died as a result of their decision. Not surprisingly, managers of the hotel had no explanation for the staff's selfless actions.[9]

This example certainly points to the power of purpose. However, research has consistently revealed that, in general, these cases are exceptional.[10] Likewise, purpose-driven companies have always been admired, regarded as something extraordinary, and, to a certain extent, anomalies of the established understanding of management. The successful cases, characterized by exceptional leaders that break the norms, have been extensively analyzed in order to understand their success. But when transferring the "good practices" from purpose-driven companies to traditional organizations, results have consistently failed to live up to that of their role models.

To that extent, it has been problematic that academics and consultants have tried to analyze and emulate purpose-driven organizations but with the wrong management logic.[11] It is like trying to see a landscape with reading glasses: you see shapes, but you miss the intimate details and the beauty of the whole. This is probably the most important insight for those who truly want to create a purpose-driven organization. Because if one uses the wrong logic, it is nearly impossible to harness the power of purpose. With a misleading logic, purpose appears to be something strange, ambiguous, and extraordinary while, in reality, it is something natural, unambiguous, and ordinary.

Purpose Demands a New Management Logic

Today, most business organizations are embedded in what scientists call the classical and neoclassical logic of management. Under such logic, organizations are seen as "machines" or "organisms" that are "designed to achieve predetermined goals in different environments."[12] It is relatively easy to see the dominance of this management logic in practice. When an employee joins an organization, for example, the basic management context that defines his or her work is established by tasks, competences, and objectives. A manager will make sure that new employees understand what to do and how to do it, but rarely does a manager truly care about **WHY** they do it.[13] One way or another, the logic goes: as long as people do their jobs, it does not really matter why they do them. However, this logic, that has driven organizations during the last century, is insufficient to understand purpose-driven organizations.

To understand purpose-driven organizations, we need to shift to a *postindustrial management logic*[14] which provides a more comprehensive view of the person and the organization. From this perspective, the meaning of work for the individual is something unique, of immense value, and is perceived as his or her deepest purpose in life. This is what some call "the anthropological" view of organizations,[15] and what we refer to here as the new management logic of purpose. In this view, a company is a place where each member's personal purpose develops, starting with that of the entrepreneur or founder, but ultimately ending with all employees. Over the last years, the seeds of this new logic have been planted in several theories of meaningful work, corporate social responsibility, authentic leadership, servant leadership, social entrepreneurship, humanistic management, and the time to benefit from all those advances is now close at hand.[16]

In this context, the old logic of management evolves into the new logic of purpose, characterized by three main traits that, we believe, will gradually become dominant in organizations (see Fig. 1.1). The first—**personal purpose**—introduces the idea of individual purpose in the organizational arena, the second—**self-management**—is the context where personal purpose flourishes within the organization, and the third—**unity**—is the natural connection between the personal and organizational purpose. Only under the lens of these three principles can organizations appreciate the true scope and beauty of a purpose-driven organization (Table 1.1).

Table 1.1 Fundamental traits of the new logic of purpose

The new logic of purpose
Personal purpose
Self-management
Unity

Personal Purpose

During the twentieth century, in a relatively stable institutional and competitive environment, the purpose of individuals within the organization was neglected in organizational theory and practice. Once organizational purpose was established by the founders or directors, employees were then expected to derive meaning and significance in their work. In this way, personal purpose was regarded implicitly subsumed by the notion of organizational purpose. Purpose development was seen primarily as a top-down exercise of charismatic leadership, creating strong and stable cultures which would define and dictate the meaning of work to individuals.

But the panorama of the twenty-first century is very different. Disrupted business models and market volatility are common place. Competitive advantage, which in the past was the cornerstone of strategy, now gives way to creating temporary and transient advantage. This requires redefining activities and organizational focus at a rate that would have been dizzying in the past. Strategy is based no longer on accurate predictions of the future, but on developing dynamic skills and capabilities that allow individuals and organizations to adapt rapidly. In this changing and uncertain world, employees no longer find solace in top-down definitions of organizational purpose. Today, more than ever, managing the tension between what people perceive as their personal purpose and the constant change required by the preferences of clients, employees, shareholders, suppliers, and other stakeholders, can be difficult.

One example of this reality comes from Barclay's CEO Antony Jenkins. Barclays, like all banks, was struggling through the financial crisis, taking its fair share of knocks. But when the Libor scandal broke, employees suffered a great loss in their sense of meaning: "that was devastating for the organization … the reactions of the society at large were very difficult to deal with … [and] the organization lost its sense of self".[17] It is clear that modern societies demand more from organizations. These new challenges, along with the increasing ambiguity we face as institutional models shift, only amplifies the loss of meaning in corporations,[18] divisions, departments, and especially, individuals within the organization.[19] Coping with external uncertainty and turbulence, organizations need to reinforce internal meaning. Because when the organization's purpose is unclear, the meaning of work for individuals severely suffers. This can be seen in the personal crises currently experienced by many professionals who find their careers meaningless, despite having reached great performance-related victories.

From this loss of personal meaning, a new paradigm has emerged: the idea of personal purpose at work. Nowadays, individual purpose can no longer be neglected or implicitly associated with organizational purpose. Employees do not wait for their companies to tell them the ultimate meaning of their work, they take the plunge and lead their own search. This is something that is generally increasing and especially prominent in our millennial generation, where a keen interest in more purposeful living as well as a shift toward collectivistic values is emerging.[20] Organizations should not fear this new reality, but on the contrary, gain an understanding of its enormous potential and implications for both the organization and the individual. Think about cases like Unilever, Medtronic, ISS Facility Services, or Telefónica—in recent years, these organizations have developed intensive programs in order to help their employees reflect on their own purpose. Without such clarity and engagement from the individual, efforts to push for an organizational purpose upon them may result in more harm than good.

The question of purpose must be raised by each employee, thus shaping the dynamism required for the organization's purpose. Companies can do this by helping each person actively search for the "why" in their work, guided by the organization's overarching "why." This is a task that is ongoing, and will require discipline to regularly reflect, revise, and update.

In addition to talking about their company's purpose, managers must learn to talk about the unique purpose of the individuals within the company, starting with their own. They should learn to "listen" and understand their employees' purpose, from the selection process onward, in order to guide its development and harmonization with the company's purpose. This connection is totally unique for each employee, as it emerges from the personal life purpose of each individual. Although some may believe the emerging presence of purpose within organizations to be a mere tactic for branding or employee engagement, we believe it is a sign of the redefinition of meaning at work that will continue to evolve in the future. This idea of connecting individual and organizational purpose, at all levels of the company, is here to stay as a necessary element for facing market environments defined by inconsistency and uncertainty.

Self-Management

Because a person's purpose is an intimate personal concept, connected to self-identity, it cannot be managed "from the outside." Attempts to dictate purpose from outside-in will come across as manipulative or paternalistic. Purpose is not something that the company grants, orders, defines, or requests. Nor does purpose derive from functional positions. Certainly, purpose is not something negotiated, as might be the case with salary or objectives. It is not the company that defines purpose for individuals, but individuals who endow their work with a purpose. In purpose, there are no bosses, superiors, orders, or chain of command.

Individuals at work discover and define the purpose of their work, and the only ones who can fully assess its scope and meaning. It is precisely this evaluation of purpose that differentiates the new logic of purpose from old management paradigms. This evaluation prompts people to reflect upon: why they exist, the point of their work, and how is the world better because of it. Under this new logic, the individual answers to these questions become the cornerstone of the purpose-driven organization. And no answer can be satisfying unless it comes "from within" in a completely free and voluntary way. The new logic of purpose requires people to lead the evolutionary process of their own purpose at work. Only then is the company truly purposeful, when employees, through the exercise of their freedom, take on the leadership of their own purpose at work, and hence they voluntarily connect with the organization's purpose.

For this reason, alongside the presence of purpose, an increasing interest has emerged in self-management[21] and job crafting[22] theories. Self-management does not mean giving up on organizational governance or hierarchy. It is about embracing a concept of freedom that means "trusting employees to think and act independently on behalf of the organization."[23] In this sense, self-management is about effectively abandoning the idea of managing people. There is a fundamental reason at play here: purpose-driven individuals do not want to be managed. In fact, they instinctively resist being managed as they know it results in lower self-expression and realization. Being managed or controlled from the outside feels unnatural, and suboptimal to free and responsible individuals, and it deters their experience of meaningful and purposeful work.

In purpose-driven organizations, maximum value comes from people who manage themselves. This was something difficult to imagine in the past, but now, with the help of technology and communication, it is a reality in many organizations. In the era of the "purpose economy,"[24] managers must be capable of facilitating self-management in their teams and allowing as much autonomy as possible within the boundaries of needed coordination and alignment.

Unity

Unity is an organizational phenomenon that results from the connection of individual purposes. When people in a group or organization share a common purpose, it generates unity between them. Sharing a common purpose, identifying with it, results in the unity of the organization.[25] A defining characteristic of unity is that it is achieved on a "person to person" basis. Every person counts. Each time an employee connects his or her personal purpose with the company purpose, the level of unity increases. Likewise, every time someone moves away from the company purpose, the level of unity decreases. Thus, fostering the development and connection of purpose within each individual greatly influences the capacity to generate organizational unity.

Take, for example, the way in which the president of Ferrer, a leading European pharmaceutical company, addressed his team: "We are not a group, we are not a corporation, we are not an assembly of companies: we are ONE." His words express the belief that unity cuts much deeper than alignment of goals and objectives, which one would expect in a group, or a corporation. Certainly, unity is related to a sense of teamwork, commitment, and collaboration—yes, these are, in part, signs of unity, but unity goes beyond this. Unity is achieved by shared connections at the level of purpose.

It is helpful to think of unity not as something that can be controlled or manipulated from the outside. It has to be fostered from within the individuals that must be united within the organization. This idea is clearly understood by companies such as Bimbo,[26] whose employees, shortly after joining, take a course to help reflect on their personal purpose and values relative to those of the company. Behind this course, attended by all of its 130,000 employees around the globe, is the founder's deep-rooted belief that[27]—"the company has a soul made by the souls of each of its workers."

It is important not to confuse unity with strategic alignment. Strategic alignment connects the "what and how" of individuals and organization through such structures as roles and incentives. Unity, on the other hand, connects the "why" of the organization and the "why" of the persons. The nature of strategic alignment is linear and mechanistic, from top to bottom, while unity of purpose is nonlinear as it emerges as much from individuals as from the organization.[28] As Bartlett and Ghoshal argue, purpose is something different from the model in which managers define strategy and put in place systems to ensure "employees toe the line."[29] Unity should not be thought of in terms of alignment from top to bottom. Rather unity should be seen as a co-creation between the organization and the individuals in it that could be represented concentrically (see Fig. 1.1). Indeed, it is no surprise that some purpose-driven organizations—e.g. Walt Disney[30]—traditionally did not display vertical hierarchical organizational charts but concentric ones.

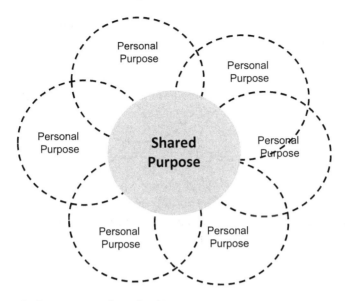

Fig. 1.1 Symbolic representation of unity

The Rise of the New Logic of Purpose

In short, we consider that the growing presence of purpose, both in companies and individuals, is an indicative sign of a new evolutionary logic of management. Like the way classical management logic prompted the division of labor, and the neoclassical logic prompted the development of organizational alignment, perhaps a new organizational theory will form, one that guides the development of the new logic of purpose within organizations. This new theory will spawn the emergence of organizational "members," those agents and individuals who identify with the organization's purpose and want to contribute toward its fulfillment. Traditional organizational boundaries will become more and more subject to question[31] and will evolve toward a wider view, based on the new logic of purpose.

But how close are we to this reality? No doubt, organizations are in different positions along the spectrum. Most mature companies, in stable markets, are closer to the old logic of management. They will need to shift as the uncertainty and ambiguity challenge their performance. And digital economy corporations such as Google, Facebook, and Amazon, which were created with ideals closer to the new logic of purpose, are influential to the movement. While many universities, hospitals, and non-profit organizations, which, quite often, have mistakenly developed under the classical and neoclassical logic, will see the new logic of purpose as a way of realizing their true spirit of purpose-driven organizations.

Although more and more companies and institutions are embracing purpose-driven practices, the true potential of this new approach is yet to be discovered. There are many challenges and obstacles that need to be overcome, and many questions yet to be answered. Exploring these questions is the aim of this book.

And in exploring them, we hope to help organizations and individuals understand how personal purpose is best developed and applied in the workplace and, most importantly, how to ensure its coherence and consistency to a given person's work. These are important questions to answer if we expect to overcome the inertia of the dominant and traditional logic of management and not succumb to the tension between purpose and the pressure of short-term financial results.

Notes

1. Hollensbe, E., Wookey, C., Hickey, L., George, G., & Nichols, C. V. (2014). Organizations with purpose. *Academy of Management Journal, 57*(5), 1227–1234.
2. See for example: Hamel, G. (2011). First, let's fire all the managers. *Harvard Business Review, 89*(12), 48–60; Craig, N., & Snook, S. (2014). From purpose to impact. *Harvard Business Review, 92*(5), 104–111; Rey, C., Chinchilla, N., & Pitta, N. (2017). Objectives are SMART, missions are WISE: Employees with purpose. *IESE Insight*, No. 33, Second Quarter 2017, pp. 45–51.
3. Grant, G. B. (2017). Exploring the possibility of peak individualism, humanity's existential crisis, and an emerging age of purpose. *Frontiers in Psychology, 8*, 1478.
4. Cardona, P., & Rey, C. (2008). *Management by missions*. New York: Palgrave Macmillan.
5. http://www.tata.com/aboutus/articlesinside/Values-and-purpose. Retrieved November 8, 2018.
6. Birkinshaw, J., Foss, N. J., & Lindenberg, S. (2014). Combining purpose with profits. *MIT Sloan Management Review, 55*(3), 49.
7. Hollensbe, E., Wookey, C., Hickey, L., George, G., & Nichols, C. V. (2014). Organizations with purpose. *Academy of Management Journal, 57*(5), 1227–1234.
8. Almandoz, J., Lee, Y., & Ribera, A. (2018). Unleashing the power of purpose: 5 steps to transform your business, *IESE Insight*, 37, Second Quarter, 44–51.

9. Deshpande, R. (2010). *Terror at the Taj Bombay: Customer-centric leadership.* Harvard Business Publishing, Multimedia/Video Case.

10. Carton, A. M., Murphy, C., & Clark, J. R. (2014). A (blurry) vision of the future: How leader rhetoric about ultimate goals influences performance. *Academy of Management Journal, 57*(6), 1544–1570.

11. Management logics are principles or paradigms that transcend a specific organization and affect the management field. They are defined as "sets of macro-level beliefs and values that strongly influence management practice and theory" and refer to "assumptions about the nature of organizations" embodied in certain dominant principles. Dijksterhuis, M. S., Van den Bosch, F. A., & Volberda, H. W. (1999). Where do new organizational forms come from? Management logics as a source of coevolution. *Organization Science, 10*(5), 569–582.

12. Dijksterhuis, M. S., Van den Bosch, F. A., & Volberda, H. W. (1999). Where do new organizational forms come from? Management logics as a source of coevolution. *Organization Science, 10*(5), 569–582.

13. Sinek, S. (2009). *Start with why: How great leaders inspire everyone to take action.* New York, NY: Penguin.

14. This logic implies that individuals at work "are able to perceive and to experience reality as a meaningful and coherent whole, giving sense to decisions and actions within the organization." Dijksterhuis, M. S., Van den Bosch, F. A., & Volberda, H. W. (1999). Where do new organizational forms come from? Management logics as a source of coevolution. *Organization Science, 10*(5), 569–582.

15. Pérez López, J. A. (2014). *Foundations of management.* Madrid: Rialp.

16. We can see the evolution of this new management logic over four stages: First, academics and practitioners pose new management principles that significantly deviate from the current state of the art. Second, the management trendsetters select certain core principles that seem promising as solutions to existing problems. Third, accompanied by social, psychological, technical, or economic changes that force the introduction of the new principle, followers are convinced of its rationality. Finally, adoption and diffusion of the new logic takes place. Abrahamson, E. (1991). Managerial fads and fashions: The diffusion and rejection of innovations. *Academy of Management Review, 16*(3), 586–612.

17. White, A., Yakis-Douglas, B., Helanummi-Cole, H., & Ventresca, M. (2017). Purpose-led organization: 'Saint Antony' reflects on the idea of organizational purpose, in principle and practice. *Journal of Management Inquiry, 26*(1), 101–107.

18. For the effect of turbulent times in purpose, ambiguity, and confusion see for example: Almandoz, J. (2012). Arriving at the starting line: The impact of community and financial logics on new banking ventures. *Academy of Management Journal, 55*(6), 1381–1406.

19. Kaplan, S. (2008). Framing contests: Strategy making under uncertainty. *Organization Science, 19*(5), 729–752.

20. Grant, G. B. (2017). Exploring the possibility of peak individualism, humanity's existential crisis, and an emerging age of purpose. *Frontiers in Psychology, 8,* 1478.

21. Laloux, F. (2014). *Reinventing organizations: A guide to creating organizations inspired by the next stage in human consciousness.* Brussels: Nelson Parker.

22. Wrzesniewski, A., LoBuglio, N., Dutton, J. E., & Berg, J. M. (2013). Job crafting and cultivating positive meaning and identity in work. In *Advances in positive organizational psychology* (pp. 281–302). London: Emerald Group Publishing Limited.

23. Gulati, R. (2018). Structure that's not stifling. *Harvard Business Review, 96*(3), 68–79.

24. Hurst, A. (2016). *The purpose economy: How your desire for impact, personal growth and community is changing the world.* Boise, ID: Elevate Publishing.

25. Melé, D. (2003). Organizational humanizing cultures: Do they generate social capital? *Journal of Business Ethics, 45*(1–2), 3–14.

26. Mexican multinational company, one of the leading food companies in the world with the purpose: "Building a sustainable, highly productive and deeply humane company."

27. Lorenzo Servitje (1918–2007).

28. Birkinshaw, J., Foss, N. J., & Lindenberg, S. (2014). Combining purpose with profits. *MIT Sloan Management Review, 55*(3), 49.

29. Bartlett, C. A., & Ghoshal, S. (1995). Changing the role of top management: Beyond systems to people. *Harvard Business Review, 73*(3), 132–142.

30. https://medium.com/the-ready/the-org-chart-is-dead-e1d76eca9ce0. Retrieved November 17, 2018.

31. Santos, F. M., & Eisenhardt, K. M. (2005). Organizational boundaries and theories of organization. *Organization Science, 16*(5), 491–508.

2

Harmonization of Personal and Organizational Purpose

Carlos Rey and Ivan Malbašić

Like most companies, Unilever has lived under a set of corporate values that have been the mainstay of the organization for decades. In 2014, inspired by these principles, the company launched a program called "Brand Purpose" with the intent of transmitting the corporate purpose across all the brands. In the same year, the company started another program called "Personal Purpose" in which it encouraged the employees, all over the world, to find their own meaning in the work they did.

Today, more than half of the Unilever brands have implemented Brand Purpose and more than 30,000 employees have participated in the personal purpose program. The internal results of the company have indicated that those brands in which purpose was implemented grew twice as fast as those which did not. And the employees who implemented their personal purpose had less burnout, greater productivity, and more innovation.

As we have seen at Unilever and many other companies, evidence from the field shows that purpose is being infused increasingly at both the corporate and the individual levels. Behind this practice is the idea of connecting individual purpose to that of the organization—what we refer to in this book

C. Rey (✉)
Universitat Internacional de Catalunya,
Barcelona, Spain
e-mail: carlosrey@uic.es

I. Malbašić
Faculty of Organization and Informatics, University of Zagreb, Zagreb, Croatia
e-mail: ivan.malbasic@foi.hr

© The Author(s) 2019
C. Rey et al. (eds.), *Purpose-driven Organizations*,
https://doi.org/10.1007/978-3-030-17674-7_2

as *unity*—making its way into companies in what clearly seems to be a constant upward trend. In this chapter, we are going to see the essence of this connection and consider its fundamental nature, along with the processes that ensure it remains vibrant over time. Built upon recent research on plural identity and authenticity at work, a two-sided view of purpose is developed, suggesting the harmonization of personal and organizational purposes across two basic dimensions: purpose fluidity and purpose synergy. The first is related to the exchange of meaningful representations between personal and organizational purposes. The second relates to the way personal and organizational purposes partly or fully integrate with each other.

Connecting the Two Sides of Purpose

Scholars typically refer to purpose from a perspective that moves *from* the organization *to* the individual, and so organizations typically define a purpose, then communicate it to their employees to offer a sense of purpose in their work. With this approach, employees need to incorporate the purpose of the organization into their own viewpoint in order to give higher meaning to their efforts. Consequently, individuals see their work as more than just a simple task, understanding it as something that contributes significantly to a higher cause. To the extent that employees internalize the organizational purpose, it affords them an opportunity to transcend the task themselves, giving them a more meaningful understanding of their work. In this regard, the organization's ultimate purpose "provides" a sense of purpose to its employees.

We can see this, for example, in the anecdote about the well-known NASA janitor who said, "I'm not mopping floors, I'm putting a man on the moon."[1] The study of this case and others investigates how leaders and their rhetoric motivate employees to internalize an organization's purpose. Like this study, much of the traditional research around purpose over recent decades has been based on this notion that purpose flows from the organization to the individual.

However, there is another side of purpose, an equally important and impactful side, that has been much less explored in management literature. It is the perspective that argues purpose must also be created and moved "*from* the individual *to* the organization." In this perspective, individuals derive a sense of meaning in their work from their personal purpose. And this plays a crucial role in the development of meaning because one's own purpose is an enormous source of motivation. It endows any task with deeper meaning, while reinforcing the individual's value system. When individuals approach their work from personal purpose, their aspirations are encouraged, and they become more energized in their current roles.[2] Personal purpose "empowers individuals with timeless strength in the midst of change."[3] More than merely fulfilling a task or doing a job, employees feel they are "being themselves at work," incorporating into the organization their unique purpose in life.

Some may think that this is attainable only for those in high positions or in vocational professions, but it is not. The work of ISS Facility Services in fostering purpose development in their employees, for instance, offers convincing examples of how one can create a higher sense of purpose even for mundane work. This is the case of the ISS cleaning professional, who works in a Næstved Municipality school in Denmark. She reflects upon her passion for serving others through her statement: "By keeping the school clean, I help the students focus on learning and developing their talents—while I do the same in my job every day." Or consider a general worker in charge of cleaning and changing the bed linen at the Tzu Chi Hospital in Taiwan who expressed his work as: "Helping patients on the way to recovery with a clean sheet." These examples challenge the understanding that some tasks have less personal meaning than the work found in professions such as medicine or education,[4] and indicate that finding meaning at work is not a matter of the kind of work you do but, rather, of the kind of person you want to be.

Such examples of purpose at work, seen in the employees referred to above, can be as powerful and meaningful as "putting a man on the moon" was for the NASA janitor. By connecting the personal purpose with work, people find a much greater understanding of the transcendence of their efforts, and more importantly, reinterpret those efforts over time.

The combination of these two notions of purpose—"from organization to individual" and "from individual to organization"—offers a more comprehensive view of the full potential of purpose in organizations. This duality of purpose not only suggests that a company "inspire" the individual, but also that a company "is inspired" by the personal purpose of each of its employees. Indeed, the purpose of the organization can provide guidance for each individual, but it should not replace the experience of every employee to discover his or her personal purpose at work.

This is consistent with research that has "demystified charismatic/transformational leadership" by demonstrating that, in purpose-driven organizations, individuals connect their work not only to the collective purpose, but also to their own personal purpose.[5] This can also be seen in the research regarding plural work identity harmonization.[6] When harmonizing purpose, individuals connect the corporate purpose with their personal purpose, finding plural sources of meaning and a sense of purpose in their daily work. Following this framework (see Table 2.1), harmonization enhances the understanding of

Table 2.1 Harmonizing purpose in organizations

Purpose harmonization	Description	Examples
Fluidity	Reinforcement between personal and organizational and purpose	• Providing employees with representations of impact to the organization and its beneficiaries • Helping employees reflect on their purpose at work • Acknowledging the purpose of each employee
Synergy	Intersection between personal and organizational purpose	• Hiring for fitting into the organizational purpose • Discovering purpose that already exists in organizational members • Designing career paths around the connection between personal and organizational purpose

how personal and organizational purposes support each other by dynamically exchanging meaning (purpose fluidity) as well as intersecting it to enrich each other (purpose synergy). This requires overcoming the "myth of two separate worlds" in which work identities are completely disconnected from non-work identities.[7] In the two-sided notion of purpose, individuals authentically receive meaning from the purpose of the organization and the organization authentically receives meaning from the purpose of each employee. It is related to what some call the "ideological currency" that enhances the psychological contract between the employee and the organization.[8]

Nurturing Fluidity

Purpose fluidity explains how individuals and organizations exchange meaningful representations of purpose at work, enhancing the sense of purpose when flowing dynamically between personal and organizational purposes. In other words, fluidity is not just using one representation of purpose (personal or organizational), but combining both at the same time, flowing from the personal to the organizational and vice versa, as is shown in Fig. 2.1. Fluidity then is based on what an organization's purpose means to the individual as well as what the individual's purpose means to the organization.

Fluidity is a powerful source of meaning and personal flourishing. It occurs when employees see and experience that contributing to the corporate purpose helps them to develop their personal purpose in life. Following the previous example, fluidity can be illustrated by such examples as "helping to put a

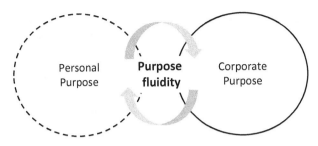

Fig. 2.1 Purpose fluidity

man on the moon reinforces my personal purpose of making an impact on society." Of course, purpose fluidity does not come by simply elaborating creative axioms, but from these connections becoming profoundly ingrained in the minds and hearts of individuals.

We have seen many practices that foster purpose fluidity. This is the case, for example, of Novo Nordisk, a company that makes medicines for diabetics, and requires that all new employees spend a day with a diabetes patient.[9] It is also the case for ISS Facility Services, where top managers spend one day a year performing frontline positions, such as cleaning or maintenance, in the premises of their clients. These practices are a source of what some call "a beneficiary contact,"[10] helping individuals to experience and gain greater consciousness of their organization's purpose.

We could offer many testimonies of people who, with pride and gratitude, refer to how such practices have helped them become both better persons and better citizens. Indeed, one of the unmistakable signs of a purpose-driven company is that, in an ordinary and sometimes unnoticed way, it positively influences the families and personal relationships of their employees. By encouraging various representations of the corporate purpose, employees find greater sources of meaning from which to choose. What does the purpose of the company in which I work mean to me? And how does it help me in the development of my purpose? These are central questions in the workshops at Bimbo, for example, where 130,000 employees reflect upon their personal purpose along with that of the organization.

Besides, fluidity is related to the question: what do various individual employee purposes mean for the company? Consider, for example, the case of KPMG. After defining the corporate purpose as "inspiring confidence and empowering change" the company did not embark on a typical slogan-based communication campaign. Instead, partners and managers, with the company's purpose as a backdrop, were encouraged to connect compelling stories and personal examples about their own purpose. Following this, the rest of the employees were invited to do the same, combining reflections on the corporate purpose with sharing their own accounts of how they believed they were making a difference. As a result of maintaining this practice over time, recruitment improved, employee turnover decreased, and the company climbed 31 places on Fortune's list of the 100 Best Companies to Work For.[11]

Fluidity requires that companies recognize the relevance of each employee's purpose. It means placing the person at the center of the organization and appreciating his or her dignity and uniqueness. In this way, fostering fluidity at scale is a means to embrace diversity in organizations, as "the idea of embedding plurality in purpose is that we share a common humanity, and people are kept at the heart of the business enterprise."[12]

Consider, for example, the business philosophy of the German company *dm-drogerie markt*[13] expressed by the motto: **"Here I'm a person. Here I'm shopping!"** Initially, it referred to their customers, but naturally started to be used to refer to the employees as well: **"Here I'm a person. Here I'm working!"** These two simple sentences are the backbone of *dm*'s business. They express the purpose of *dm*, that is, respect for people, or more precisely, respect for the value and uniqueness of each individual. *dm* explains this motto by stating that it is a commitment to put the individual at the center of everything, whether he/she is a customer or a worker, offering to every person the right to emphasize his/her individuality. For *dm*, embracing diversity is much more than a matter of quotas, but of respecting each individual as he or she is.[14]

Fluidity allows individuals to connect personal and organizational purposes without necessarily identifying them. This is especially relevant for the many positions and professions that are not commonly thought of as professional, such as the worker in a factory or the cashier at a supermarket. This is because fluidity is based on concordance,[15] and refers to the extent to which the organizational purpose can be used by employees to express their authentic interests and values.

We observed this reality in the practice of a store manager at Decathlon, which he called "the 15 minutes of purpose" meeting. At the beginning of each day, store employees gathered and exchange tales and anecdotes from the previous day about how they promoted the corporate purpose of "making sport accessible to many" (e.g., how an employee helped advise a customer on how to best prepare for a triathlon, or helped another customer find the best bicycle for his particular needs). However, we saw in many cases, that more enthusiasm was expressed for stories not related to sports but rather, to other themes that were significant to the one explaining it (e.g., "I helped a young boy find a good present for his girlfriend"; "I made a sad client have a good time shopping in the store"). Speaking with the employees, we observed that, even the ones who were not very passionate about sports, by making meaningful connections of their personal purposes with the company's purpose, gained a better sense of purpose in their activities.

Keeping the dynamic fluidity "alive" is about what some have called "making every-day-work meaningful."[16] And since fluidity goes in two directions, it is much like friendship or trust. We can trust someone, but if we do not feel that person's corresponding trust in us, our own trust will be short lived. The same happens with purpose fluidity. If individuals do not see that the organization values their personal purpose in life, sooner than later they will become distant to their organization's purpose and purpose fluidity will be lost.

Facilitating Synergy

When a company hires someone, it hires much more than a particular set of knowledge and skills. A person's greatest potential lies in his or her personal life's purpose, in the enthusiasm and determination through which he or she wants to contribute to the betterment of society. It is a desire that exceeds the field of labor, but does not at all exclude it. The desire we all have to make a difference and contribute to make a better world is a company's true source of innovation and creativity, and represents the key to our willingness to constantly improve ourselves, whether that be in knowledge or skill. The greatest asset of an organization is the personal purpose of each individual and one's aspiration to be useful and to leave a mark. Many companies are well aware of this reality and harness it. Consider, for example, how the Indian IT services HCL Technologies promotes what they call the Employee Passion Indicator Count (EPIC), which is used to identify the key "passions" of employees and to steer them toward jobs where these could be put to best use.[17]

Purpose synergy is found at the junction of company purpose and personal purpose (see Fig. 2.2). Purpose synergy is the place of overlap between the

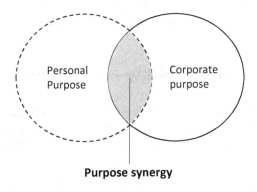

Purpose synergy

Fig. 2.2 Purpose synergy

company and the individual, where the interests of the company and its individual employees combine to reach its most perfect form. It is not a simple exercise in self-development, one that is disconnected from the company purpose. Nor is it an exercise in indoctrinating employees with the corporate purpose. It is not about training courses or communication campaigns. It is about channeling the potential of the person's purpose within the context of the company's purpose. Purpose synergy reveals what the person best brings to the company and vice versa. Thus, synergy occurs in part of the company purpose as well as the individual's life purpose.

Consider, for example, the case of Alpha Omega, a high-tech medical device company in Israel devoted to the purpose of improving peoples' lives. Its founders, Imad and Reem Younis, have been committed, from a very young age, to the purpose of developing work environments where Jews and Arabs can work together in harmony. And in leading their company, they incorporate this personal purpose into the corporate purpose. They hire Jews and Arabs alike, employees who not only excelled at their work, but also share in a dream of creating inclusive work environments. At Alpha Omega, the purpose of improving peoples' lives is defined as "Joined together to improve people's life," creating a strong synergy between organizational purpose and the personal purpose of the founders and employees. As Imad has said, "it is like putting my soul inside the company's soul."[18]

When organizations develop purpose synergy, employees find more energy and sense of purpose in their work, and feel like "putting their soul into their work." One way to create synergy is by recruiting employees who have personal affinities with the organizational purpose. Especially when creating new companies, this is one of the most powerful ways to create synergy. Another way, especially relevant in the case of existing employees, is to find and foster a purpose that already exists in the organization. Following the principle of "If it is real, it is possible," it is about "finding examples of people or teams within the organization that exceed the norms, examining the purpose that drives their excellence, and then imagining it imbuing the entire workforce."[19]

The Joint Effect of Fluidity and Synergy

Fluidity and synergy have common drivers, but are different from each other. Fluidity allows the connecting of personal and organizational purposes without necessarily identifying solely with one or the other. With synergy, however, both personal and organizational purposes partly or fully identify with one another, meaning that the organization incorporates the purpose of the individuals and vice versa. We could say that fluidity helps organizational and personal purposes get closer, while synergy integrates them. Fluidity helps to create unity, synergy is the result of the unity itself.

But together with these fundamental practices, synergy must be reinforced and sustained by constant fluidity. Because if employees do not flow at work, even the existing synergy can be snuffed out. Fluidity helps not only to create synergy, but also to sustain it and keep it alive. This explains why, despite recruiting people who have a great affinity for the corporate purpose, synergy will not occur if employees, for example, see that the organization is not true to its purpose or if they feel that the organization does not respect the dignity and uniqueness of employees' purpose. And this can happen even in professional jobs, like those of doctors or teachers, where purpose synergy usually comes as part and parcel with the profession.

In short, the phenomenon of shared purpose is an inspiration for both individuals and organizations. Employees should continually seek what is, or what could inspire them at work, embracing a deeper understanding—that the purpose of their work is much more than earning a salary or having good working conditions. Companies, on the other side, should see their employees not just as human capital or means of return, but as individuals with invaluable potential with different ideas and personalities that provide an inexhaustible source of creativity. And the responsibility for connecting purpose lies with both—organizations need to be truly interested in what their employees want to contribute to the world, while at the same time employees should see their work as a way to fulfill collective aspirations and dreams.

Notes

1. Carton, A. M. (2018). "I'm not mopping the floors, I'm putting a man on the moon": How NASA leaders enhanced the meaningfulness of work by changing the meaning of work. *Administrative Science Quarterly, 63*(2), 323–369.
2. Craig, N., & Snook, S. (2014). From purpose to impact. *Harvard Business Review, 92*(5), 104–111.
3. Covey, S. R. (1989). *The 7 habits of highly effective people: Powerful lessons in personal change.* New York, NY: Fireside/Simon & Schuster.
4. Ariely, D., Kamenica, E., & Prelec, D. (2008). Man's search for meaning: The case of Legos. *Journal of Economic Behavior & Organization, 67*(3–4), 671–677.
5. Bono, J. E., & Judge, T. A. (2003). Self-concordance at work: Toward understanding the motivational effects of transformational leaders. *Academy of Management Journal, 46*(5), 554–571.

6. This framework explains that authenticity at work occurs in two sequential processes. The first, synchronization, is about the way individuals understand their own work within the available organizational identities (e.g., "putting a man on the moon"). The second, harmonization, is related to how individuals understand their work combining self-identities (e.g., "I want to make an impact on society") and organizational identities. Harmonization enhances the understanding of how the work and self-identities dynamically exchange meaning ("identity fluidity") and how they enrich each other ("identity synergy"). Caza, B. B., Moss, S., & Vough, H. (2017). From synchronizing to harmonizing: The process of authenticating multiple work identities. *Administrative Science Quarterly, 63*(4), 703–745.

7. Ramarajan, L., & Reid, E. (2013). Shattering the myth of separate worlds: Negotiating nonwork identities at work. *Academy of Management Review, 38*(4), 621–644.

8. Thompson, J. A., & Bunderson, J. S. (2003). Violations of principle: Ideological currency in the psychological contract. *Academy of Management Review, 28*(4), 571–586.

9. Birkinshaw, J., Foss, N. J., & Lindenberg, S. (2014). Combining purpose with profits. *MIT Sloan Management Review, 55*(3), 49.

10. Grant, A. M. (2012). Leading with meaning: Beneficiary contact, prosocial impact, and the performance effects of transformational leadership. *Academy of Management Journal, 55*(2), 458–476.

11. Quinn, R. E., & Thakor, A. V. (2018, July–August). Creating a purpose-driven organization. *Harvard Business Review*, pp. 78–85.

12. Hollensbe, E., Wookey, C., Hickey, L., George, G., & Nichols, C. V. (2014). Organizations with purpose. *Academy of Management Journal, 57*(5), 1227–1234.

13. One of the largest drug chains in Central and South-Eastern Europe, established in 1973 in Karlsruhe, Germany, that sells cosmetics, healthcare items, household products, and health food.

14. There are many interesting aspects of purpose fluidity at dm. One fascinating part is the story about the founder and owner of dm. Just when everybody thought that he had done everything possible for his "capitalism with a human face," the world was astonished to learn that he had decided to leave his fortune not to his children (and he had seven!), but to give it away for charitable purposes. This resonates even more when one realizes that his wealth is estimated at more than a billion euros. This amazing decision was for him reasonable, as it was based on a principle deeply ingrained in his personal purpose: "There is no shame in becoming rich, but it is a shame to die rich."

15. Sheldon, K. M., & Elliot, A. J. (1999). Goal striving, need satisfaction, and longitudinal well-being: The self-concordance model. *Journal of Personality and Social Psychology, 76*(3), 482.

16. Almandoz, J., Lee, Y., & Ribera, A. (2018). Unleashing the power of purpose: 5 steps to transform your business, *IESE Insight*, 37, Second Quarter, 44–51.
17. Birkinshaw, J., Foss, N. J., & Lindenberg, S. (2014). Combining purpose with profits. *MIT Sloan Management Review*, 55(3), 49.
18. https://www.youtube.com/watch?v=ejLoKiBzL94&t=237s.   Retrieved January 30, 2019.
19. Quinn, R. E., & Thakor, A. V. (2018, July–August). Creating a purpose-driven organization. *Harvard Business Review*, pp. 78–85.

3

Three Dimensions of Purpose: Knowledge, Motivation, and Action

Carlos Rey and Miquel Bastons

During a strategy class on the subject of purpose, a student approached the professor and said: "Look at this article, it says that in this company people dance at meetings and in their office they have pool tables, foosball, X-Box ... the whole company is decorated as if it were a beach in the Caribbean, because it is the place where all the employees affirmed that they would like to work." The professor was intrigued by this company and decided to invite its CEO to his classroom. The CEO agreed and shared with the students how he was trying to create a great culture within his organization. He told them about the importance of having a purpose, of the sense of work, of inner balance, of being comfortable with oneself. He told them about the games in the office, the Caribbean decor, and dancing at meetings. Once his presentation was over, a student asked: Could you explain to us your business? The man explained that he had 70 stores, 300 employees, a warehouse, and he was in the process of giving more details, but then came a second question: one of the students asked what is the reason for the dancing, does it somehow contribute to the business? He replied: no, we don't really do this for the business. Then came a third question, about the 70 stores: Do the 300 workers there also dance and have foosball, PlayStation, and pool tables? Well, no, they don't. The stores have to take care

C. Rey (✉)
Universitat Internacional de Catalunya,
Barcelona, Spain
e-mail: carlosrey@uic.es

M. Bastons
Department of Economy and Business Organization, Universitat Internacional de Catalunya, Barcelona, Spain
e-mail: bastons@uic.es

© The Author(s) 2019
C. Rey et al. (eds.), *Purpose-driven Organizations*,
https://doi.org/10.1007/978-3-030-17674-7_3

of our customers. And finally came the most important question; in a respectful but incisive tone a student asked: what do you tell your store employees when they read in the press that their colleagues in headquarters are dancing and playing pool and X-Box? Just then, the teacher looked at the time and said: well, the class is over! After two weeks, the professor distributed a survey to this company's employees, in order to assess how they internalized the organization's purpose. Did they understand and share in the purpose? Interestingly, their results were among the worst in a broader study of 200 companies.

The following year the teacher ran across a good friend who told him: I know a CEO whom you should meet, he has recently remodeled the entire office. It now includes pool tables, foosball, and yoga spaces … they even gave it a name … they call it the "optimist building." As a precaution, before inviting the CEO, the professor distributed the same survey on purpose internalization. The results were impressive: This company ranked as one of the highest in the survey of all 200 companies. The following Friday, the CEO arrived to class. He showed a single slide. It read: "The Purpose of the Organization" and under it were listed many concepts that, at first glance, might seem to be a disconnected hodgepodge of lofty ideals and hard-headed results. Things like: market share, the sense of work, productivity, love for customers, return on investment, happiness of the workers, social concern, cost control, purpose, strategy, optimism, efficiency. He greeted the students and said: "I'm going to talk about the purpose of my company," and for an hour and a half he explained how he connected "everything" to "everything." As he talked, it was hard not to notice his deep authenticity, coherence, and integrity in everything he discussed about the business. This was one of the best lessons about purpose they had ever received.

In recent years, we have seen an increasing interest in academic research about purpose both in individuals[1] and in organizations.[2] Benefits of purpose have been found, for example, in areas as diverse as health, well-being, work productivity, learning, innovation, and financial performance.[3] In pursuit of these and other benefits, companies invest time and effort in devising an elaborate and well-crafted corporate purpose that articulates, for the public, their core values and main goals. However, the most challenging task is to create a purpose that really touches the hearts and minds of the employees, makes them feel proud of being part of the company, and leads to shared ambitions.[4] Contemporary organizations need to create an effective purpose that is successful in eliciting the emotional commitment of the employees. This process is not about designing a statement that will be printed on organizational documents, but rather one that will be imprinted in the heads—and especially the hearts—of employees. Defining and communicating such an effective purpose is not an easy task.

Table 3.1 Examples of 'linear' frameworks for purpose development

Frameworks for purpose development based on steps, phases, or stages	Source
Purpose Value Chain 1. Align strategy with purpose 2. Develop organizational capabilities 3. Design a resource architecture consistent with purpose 4. Establish management systems to support the purpose	Trevor & Varcoe (2017)
How to Balance Strategy and Purpose 1. Know your purpose 2. Aim for the golden mean 3. Develop corporate plasticity 4. Actively lead operationalization	Chevreux, Lopez, Mesnard (2017)
Unleashing the Power of Purpose 1. Set a clear mission and measure it 2. Foster consistent culture through people management 3. Focus on making every daily work meaningful 4. Pay attention to peripheries 5. Cultivate better managers	Almandoz, Lee, & Ribera (2018)
Creating a Purpose-Driven Organization 1. Envision an inspired workforce 2. Discover the purpose 3. Recognize the need for authenticity 4. Turn the authentic message into a constant message 5. Stimulate individual learning 6. Turn mid-level managers into purpose-driven leaders 7. Connect the people to the purpose 8. Unleash the positive energizers	Quinn & Thakor (2018)

Trevor, J., & Varcoe, B. (2017). How aligned is your organization? *Harvard Business Review Digital Articles*, pp. 2–6; Chevreux, L., Lopez, J., & Mesnard, X. (2017). The best companies know how to balance strategy and purpose. *Harvard Business Review Digital Articles*; Almandoz, J., Lee, Y., & Ribera, A. (2018). Unleashing the power of purpose: 5 steps to transform your business, *IESE Insight*, 37, Second Quarter, 44–51; Quinn, R. E., & Thakor, A. V. (2018, July–August). Creating a purpose-driven organization. *Harvard Business Review*, pp. 78–85.

It is no surprise that a plethora of new books and articles have recently appeared to help guide companies on their way to becoming purpose-driven organizations. From the theoretical and practitioner side, there are new frameworks developing as a result of the analysis being done on successful purpose-driven companies like McDonald's, Walt Disney, Apple, and others (see Table 3.1).

These frameworks, elaborated by academics and consultants, analyze purpose under the lens of linear logic using steps, phases, or sequential stages.

Not by coincidence, this nicely resembles the classical three-step strategic planning framework of analyze, design, and execute, built, as well, on linear logic. To a certain extent, there is wisdom in this perspective, as academics and consultants need to sell their ideas, which usually are easier to convey when they are explained through linear reasoning. Such frameworks certainly capture learning from the field and highlight important tips for developing purpose-driven organizations.

However, the linear approach has relevant limitations. It can lead to the misleading belief that successful cases of purpose-driven organizations like Apple or Walt Disney are the consequence of a linear movement that goes from "A" to "B." But purpose is not of that nature. From recent research on purpose, we know that the linear approach can significantly harm purpose development, especially its effective internalization and consistency. This is due to the fact that the development of purpose commonly requires balancing multiple objectives (e.g. prosocial and economic goals),[5] that are not entirely compatible with one another, "which makes a simple linear approach very hard to sustain."[6] Purpose development requires an "oblique" approach that provides causal explanations between concepts that apparently may be considered disconnected.[7] An example of oblique logic is "purpose first, profits second." Instead of indicating a linear relationship, it establishes an indirect relationship. Another example could be: "first give, then receive," on which many companies have built their purpose (e.g. Mercadona[8]), or the one of DaVita[9]: "community first, company second." Here, purpose development is primarily based on an oblique logic, especially relevant when the different objectives of the company are not entirely compatible. It is consistent with what some call "to put things in proper order": when purpose is achieved, monetary benefits can be its natural outcome.[10] As Ratan Tata, former CEO of the Tata Group, has observed, "you can make money by doing good things rather than the other way around."[11]

We invite you to make a simple experiment. Go to any company you know with a really embedded purpose, where it emerged naturally. When you speak with the people, they will rarely tell you things like: "We first defined the purpose, second we enculturated it and then we articulated it." Instead, they will describe stories, living tales, and anecdotes, all full of oblique logic. In the personal sphere, you can do a similar exercise when encountering people who naturally live their personal purpose in life (or simply think about how you do it yourself). More than linear frameworks, you will discover a lot of oblique reasoning. "Put family and friends first and good things will come," is an example obtained from the CEO of a successful high-tech company when asked how he maintains his purpose in life.

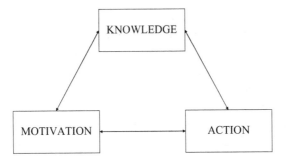

Fig. 3.1 3D model of purpose (Based on Rey, C., & Bastons, M. (2018). Three dimensions of effective mission implementation. *Long Range Planning, 51*, 580–585)

The conceptual and practical understanding of purpose development should not be formed in linear reasoning. But rather, think of it as more related to what some call "practical wisdom," that "synthesizes 'knowing why' with 'knowing how' with 'knowing what'."[12] So, frameworks based on linear logic alone do not lead to effective implementation of purpose, because the nature of purpose is not linear. The nature of purpose is formed by three unique yet interrelated components: knowledge, action, and motivation (see Fig. 3.1). The first dimension, *knowledge*, represents the explicit understanding members have about an organization's purpose. The second, *action*, reflects the practical fulfillment of purpose. And finally, *motivation*, the most intimate side of the purpose, is represented by the deep needs found in every one of us.

Purpose as Knowledge

For purpose to develop, individuals need to know it, and be able to express it in their own words. In this regard, purpose is related to what is commonly called "the purpose statement." That is, for example, the definition of purpose by Bartlett and Ghoshal as "the statement of a company's moral response to its broadly defined responsibilities."[13] From this perspective, purpose can be viewed as a *formal* commitment, one which embraces social needs and problems, and not as some platitude regarding social responsibility or an abstract idea pointed at satisfying specific stakeholder needs. It is understood as the reason for the being of the business itself.

Many researchers have recognized the importance of having *explicit knowledge* around purpose. For example, when relating purpose to profits, scholars distinguished between "purpose camaraderie" and "purpose clarity," where only the second is associated with better results.[14] And having clarity of purpose helps both organizations and individuals alike, especially in times of uncertainty and turbulence, when individual decisions and actions are more easily blown off course. Purpose cannot be taken for granted. It has to be at the forefront of consciousness. Its presence can transform a firm, but its loss can destroy an institution.[15]

It is important to recognize that organizational purpose can be greatly influenced by the living principles of the founder, like Starbucks: "to inspire and nurture the human spirit" is an extension of Howard Schultz's beliefs. But for many, purpose is the result of a true north developed and formed over time. There is a certain paradox to this: *purpose is formed over time and through changing circumstances, and yet, once clarified, it does not change with time or circumstances.* This is why, when organizations reflect on purpose, they must look toward its essence and the fundamental meaning that has always been present, and has endured the test of time. Questions like—*what does your company stand for? What was the original founding philosophy? How would society be worse off or different without your company?*—can be a good way to start discovering the purpose.[16]

Purpose as Action

The idea that purpose encompasses action is relatively intuitive. An organization can reinforce its purpose once it is written, but the significance of purpose is not limited by the boundaries of the purpose statement. Similar to the way in which the knowledge of purpose is made explicit through statements, purpose as action is made explicit through its operational development. Consider, for example, the internet eyewear retailer Warby Parker, where the company's purpose—"to do good"—is extended in actions like ensuring for every pair of glasses sold, a pair is distributed to someone in need.[17]

Indeed, this second understanding of purpose—as action—provides a different approach to the concept of purpose. We could say that, with regard to knowledge, the nature of purpose is formal and static—focused on the statement and its content. While with regard to action, the purpose becomes dynamic. What matters in the latter, is not just the content of the statement but the degree or extent to which the company is putting into practice what it says in its purpose statement. And in this way, purpose becomes something related not only to some specific actions, but to the whole activity of the company. Thus, purpose must be applied to all the arenas in which the company performs its activities and makes its decisions.

The relevance of purpose as action and its influence on meaning can be seen in recent findings that invite us to consider how leaders inspire employees not only through the words they use to link work to purpose, but also through their actions that redesign work.[18] This approach is in line with several authors' proposals to evaluate the performance relative to purpose and to express purpose in terms of specific results.[19] Indeed, the purpose statement is merely an intellectual exercise, but you need the systems and procedures to bring it to life. It is related to how the companies measure their success beyond the mere economic or financial results. This is for example the case of DaVita; following the principle of "we say, we did," the company measures every outcome it can to assess how well their purpose is becoming a reality.[20]

Using measures and indicators to evaluate purpose requires one to accept the tension between saying on the one hand "you cannot manage what you don't measure" and on the other, "there are important things that you cannot measure but you need to manage." Purpose measurement requires using metrics to evaluate its fulfillment but also understanding that the legitimacy of measurement is always sustained by the purpose itself. And when measurement becomes the end in itself, it detracts from the sense of purpose. This was nicely labeled by a manager of one company as "Indicator-itis." After some years of measuring their purpose according to a set of indicators, he observed that some of his managers were confusing indicators with the purpose itself. Another example of "Indicator-itis" can be seen in the findings of Insead Professor Quy Huy in his analysis of the fall of Nokia. Rather than focusing on the purpose, "top managers were afraid of the external environment and not meeting their quarterly targets."[21] Purpose metrics must be dynamic, helping to express the purpose based on both the external realities of markets and the internal conditions of the organization.

Purpose as Motivation

Knowledge and action reflect two basic interrelated dimensions of purpose. However, to understand the true essence of purpose we need to consider a third dimension, one that draws on the beliefs and motivations of the individual.[22] Consider, for example, the case of an area director at ISS Facility services, a European company with more than 3000 employees. Every year this director gathers his team for a one-day meeting in which they discuss their strategy, results, objectives, and action plans. In the last meeting, however, he opened with a proposal that surprised everyone: "this year we are not going to dedicate the day to reviewing how we fulfill our purpose, rather we are going to devote the whole day to reflect on how we *feel* the purpose in our lives."

When purpose touches the heart of a person, it becomes a great source of energy that helps one to transcend their own interest, further fueling the fulfillment of purpose.[23] Considering purpose solely from the perspective of a statement or the purposeful action simplifies the concept of purpose. In practice, a purpose such as "improve people's lives" certainly carries the implicit purpose "to ensure that employees are personally motivated to improve people's lives." Although, improving people's lives, this is not their true purpose if the only motivation of the organization is to make money. As stated by IESE Business School professors, "If the only motivation of purpose is because it might make you more money, then you really need to ask yourself whether your motivation is right in the first place."[24] Purpose boost profits only if it is pursued for its own sake.[25] Indeed, in our experience, this is the root cause of most of the failures we have seen: the "purpose of the purpose" was not the purpose.

Internalization, Implementation, and Integration

The way genuine purpose is nurtured in organizations nicely resembles a spiral, turning around a fixed point or center. When companies are true to their purpose, the three dimensions of purpose approach each other and *knowledge*, *motivation*, and *action* become unified. This is the main difference between the linear approach of purpose and the oblique approach that we will describe and build throughout this book. It is not simply about doing things to develop purpose, no, it is placing purpose as the central point around which all else turns. That means developing the three dimensions of purpose in a concurrent and harmonious fashion. If we develop only one or two without the other(s), the purpose suffers.

We have seen many examples of this in the marketplace. Take Aigües de Barcelona, a water supply company. Inspired by their purpose: "committed to people, we care for our water and build the city" the management team launched a program with 20 purpose-driven projects deployed throughout the organization. However, after one year the results were disappointing. It was not until they started fostering internalization of the purpose in middle managers and employees that they saw these projects providing greatly improved results. From this experience, they realized that, as one manager declared, "for purpose to be a reality, the purpose must be loved." This and many other experiences show that it is necessary to place an intermediate element between knowledge and practice: purpose must be loved and internalized by organizational members. Therefore, purpose development needs a three-dimensional approach, integrating simultaneously knowledge with motivation (internalization), knowledge with action (implementation), and motivation with action (integration) (Fig. 3.2).

Purpose internalization is the connection between the knowledge of purpose and the motivation. It is the process through which organizational members "buy into" the purpose of the company, incorporating it in their beliefs and motivations. No doubt, the first to benefit from internalization is the company itself, as it is the basis on which unity is built. Purpose internalization is what turns purpose—such as "promote well-being in society"—from an abstraction into something truly sought after by its members. Without this, we could say that purpose does not exist. In other words, to understand the "why" of an organization, we must consider the "why" of each member within the organization, as well as their underlying motivations.

The internalization of purpose creates this link by reflecting a person's motivations relative to the fulfillment of purpose. It is the development of these motivations that go beyond economic incentives (extrinsic motivations) and self-satisfaction (intrinsic motivations). They aim at meeting the needs of

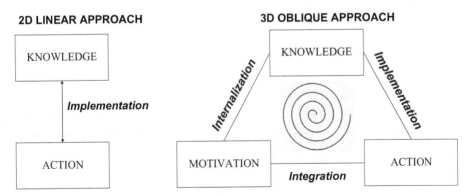

Fig. 3.2 Linear and oblique approach for purpose development

others and, therefore, depend on "pro-others motivation," identified in the research as "prosocial motivation."[26] Naturally, purpose internalization should be sought among employees in the first place, but it may also be found in other agents who act as "contributing agents" to the fulfillment of purpose. An example of this can be found in the efforts companies make to incorporate their customers, suppliers, and shareholders into their purpose. Think about, for example, the case of Aigües de Barcelona. They take significant effort in making their customers (the citizens) conscious of the sustainable use of water, motivating them to use better water management practices.

Purpose implementation is the connection between the knowledge of purpose and the action. When a company effectively implements purpose, it can be seen in the contributions it makes to society and to the people around it. Purpose implementation has two basic expressions. The first looks back in time to the degree in which a company's practices correspond to its purpose, ultimately looking to answer the question "how are we fulfilling our purpose?" The second looks toward the future and involves expressing the purpose in terms of events and results that must be achieved going forward. In this regard, expressing purpose in concrete actions and results becomes part of the purpose implementation itself. What matters then is the extent to which the company fulfills *and* intends to fulfill its formal purpose—what the company has done and intends to do. The importance of purpose, then, translates to a practical realm by guiding the company in aspects such as defining strategy, communicating objectives, or making tactical choices. Implementing purpose through the challenges and activities we deal with daily ultimately helps enhance the meaning of work. Purpose implementation provides clarity and confidence, helping employees to stay the course and remaining true to the essence of the organization. Implementation and internalization must always go hand in hand, developed in a simultaneous fashion. Advances in purpose implementation without internalization risk failing over time, being perceived as inauthentic strategy development, or simply incoherent with regard to the organization's professed purpose.

Purpose integration is the natural connection between the motivation and the action. This integration is the result of combining implementation and internalization in a natural way. It is about transforming purpose into a "habit" that is performed on a regular basis in harmony with the individuals' motivations. It is earned over time and stimulates the ability to transform purpose into everyday action. In some way, integration is the quality of placing purpose in everything we do, both in the most significant and in the most commonplace. Purpose integration is what differentiates for example, a sales person that makes a sale simply to cover the budget, from the sales person that makes a sale for the betterment of a client. Purpose integration reflects the purity of intention in our daily tasks and objectives, and helps build trustworthy and lasting relationships between the company and its stakeholders. Likewise, we see a lack of integration when companies talk in platitudes and altruisms (like we see with too many CSR programs), but fail to integrate purpose into their daily practices or when they make unnecessary use of economic incentives for activities that already carry a prosocial motivation.

These three processes—internalization, implementation, and integration—do not form a linear model. They are not sequential steps, phases, or stages, nor is there a direct cause-effect relationship between them. But rather, these three processes are tied by an oblique (or indirect) relationship: one cannot be properly developed without the others, and they must be developed simultaneously, when trying to apply them in the daily life of the organization. The spiral depicted by the incremental and simultaneous development of the three processes makes the difference between simply implementing a "purpose plan" and consistently striving to be true to your company's purpose over time. It shows how purpose-driven companies connect "everything to everything," because they connect everything to purpose.

Notes

1. Grant, G. B. (2017). Exploring the possibility of peak individualism, humanity's existential crisis, and an emerging age of purpose. *Frontiers in Psychology,* *8,* 1478.
2. Hollensbe, E., Wookey, C., Hickey, L., George, G., & Nichols, C. V. (2014). Organizations with purpose. *Academy of Management Journal,* *57*(5), 1227–1234.
3. For a review of purpose benefits see: Yemiscigil, A. (2018). *Purpose: A new paradigm with implications for policy, business, and individual lives.* Unpublished manuscript, Istanbul: Global Relations Forum.
4. Carton, A. M., Murphy, C., & Clark, J. R. (2014). A (blurry) vision of the future: How leader rhetoric about ultimate goals influences performance. *Academy of Management Journal,* *57*(6), 1544–1570.
5. Porter, M. E., & Kramer, M. R. (2006). The link between competitive advantage and corporate social responsibility. *Harvard Business Review,* *84*(12), 78–92.
6. Birkinshaw, J., Foss, N. J., & Lindenberg, S. (2014). Combining purpose with profits. *MIT Sloan Management Review,* *55*(3), 49–56.
7. Foss, N. J., & Lindenberg, S. (2013). Microfoundations for strategy: A goal-framing perspective on the drivers of value creation. *Academy of Management Perspectives,* *27*(2), 85–102.

8. Leading distribution company in Spain.

9. American healthcare company.

10. Almandoz, J., Lee, Y., & Ribera, A. (2018). Unleashing the power of purpose: 5 steps to transform your business, *IESE Insight*, 37, Second Quarter, 44–51.

11. Birkinshaw, J., Foss, N. J., & Lindenberg, S. (2014). Combining purpose with profits. *MIT Sloan Management Review, 55*(3), 49–56.

12. Nonaka, I., Chia, R., Holt, R., & Peltokorpi, V. (2014). *Wisdom, management and organization. Management Learning, 45*(4), 365–376.

13. Bartlett, C. A., & Ghoshal, S. (1993). Beyond the M-form: Toward a managerial theory of the firm. *Strategic Management Journal, 14*(S2), 23–46.

14. Gartenberg, C., Prat, A., & Serafeim, G. (2019). Corporate purpose and financial performance. *Organization Science*.

15. Mourkogiannis, N. (2014). *Purpose: The starting point of great companies*. New York: St. Martin's Press.

16. Arena, C. (2007). *The high purpose company*. Jakarta: Gramedia Pustaka Utama.

17. Gulati, R. (2018). Structure that's not stifling. *Harvard Business Review, 96*(3), 68–79.

18. Grant, A. M. (2012). Leading with meaning: Beneficiary contact, prosocial impact, and the performance effects of transformational leadership. *Academy of Management Journal, 55*(2), 458–476.

19. Rey, C., & Bastons, M. (2018). Three dimensions of effective mission implementation. *Long Range Planning, 51*(4), 580–585.

20. Almandoz, J., Lee, Y., & Ribera, A. (2018). Unleashing the power of purpose: 5 steps to transform your business, *IESE Insight*, 37, Second Quarter, 44–51.

21. Huy, Q., & Vuori, T. (2015, September 22). Who killed Nokia? Nokia did. *INSEAD Knowledge*.

22. Rey, C., & Bastons, M. (2018). Three dimensions of effective mission implementation. *Long Range Planning, 51*(4), 580–585.

23. Campbell, A., & Nash, L. L. (1992). *A sense of mission: Defining direction for the large corporation*. Reading, MA: Addison-Wesley Longman.

24. Almandoz, J., Lee, Y., & Ribera, A. (2018). Unleashing the power of purpose: 5 steps to transform your business, *IESE Insight*, 37, Second Quarter, 44–51.

25. Mourkogiannis, N. (2014). *Purpose: The starting point of great companies*. New York: St. Martin's Press.

26. Grant, A. M. (2007). Relational job design and the motivation to make a prosocial difference. *Academy of Management Review, 32*(2), 393–417.

4

Why Purpose Needs Strategy (and Vice Versa)

Carlos Rey and Joan E. Ricart

*An independent director once had to deal with a conflict on his board when a strategy consultant presented a report after three months of intensive analysis. According to the **consultant**, the only feasible scenario was to abandon the company's main customer base and move into a new market segment altogether. This would entail considerable downsizing of the company. The report was based on a thorough and consistent analysis of the company's market share distribution, as well as, demographic trends, economies of scale, and many other statistics. The report was impeccable. It was so well argued and supported by data that it seemed impossible that anything other than the consultant's proposal would be considered. However, none of it made sense to the **CEO**. His main argument was emphatic: "I don't see how we can do this. Moving to this new market segment is a big leap from our traditional business. We've successfully run this company for over 20 years, and we've always known where to focus our efforts. This proposal doesn't fit at all with the idea that I have for this business. I'm not completely against downsizing if strictly necessary, but moving into this new segment? Sorry guys, I simply don't see it."*

C. Rey (✉)
Universitat Internacional de Catalunya,
Barcelona, Spain
e-mail: carlosrey@uic.es

J. E. Ricart
Strategic Management Department, IESE Business School, Barcelona, Spain
e-mail: JERicart@iese.edu

© The Author(s) 2019
C. Rey et al. (eds.), *Purpose-driven Organizations*,
https://doi.org/10.1007/978-3-030-17674-7_4

43

*Next, the **president** took the floor: "We cannot accept this under any circumstance. We must remain faithful to the values that have been the beacon of this company for years. Consultants need to understand that we are a family-owned company, not a public company that looks only to maximizing profits. The best thing to do is to stay true to ourselves and do the right thing. The consultant's advice for us to fire employees would entail the opposite."*

When he got home, the independent director reviewed his notes and became more and more concerned. The next board meeting would be held in three days and he needed something more concrete to propose. Each member had his own arguments, and he could not see how to frame a plausible course of action. He left his notes and took a deep breath while asking himself: "So, who's right?"

Despite decades of research on strategy, "we still know little about what strategy means to actual strategists and how they use it in practice."[1] Indeed, there is an increasing concern that most management theories are not relevant to practice because they are unable to capture the "logic of practice."[2] In the real world, organizations rarely embrace a single logic. Both organizations and individuals face and maintain coexisting multiple logic that "may or may not be mutually compatible."[3]

This pluralistic view of strategy can be explained by what we call the multi-logic of strategy. The strategic logic is a set of macro-level beliefs and schemas that strongly influence both strategic theory and practice, and refer to assumptions about the nature of strategic choices. As the concept of strategy has the potential to help us explain "how the relationship between managerial cognition and managerial practice leads to organizational outcomes,"[4] the concept of strategic logic helps us to understand how different kinds of logic may affect how managers understand strategy.

At the intersection of cognitive and strategic management theories, we identify three salient sources of strategic logic—the analytical, business model, and institutional perspectives, each one forming a different perspective of strategy (see Table 4.1). The first entails the procedures used by managers to understand reality, the second has to do with business model creation and development, and the third is related to the role of companies in society and their business environment.

Table 4.1 Analytical, business model, and institutional perspectives

Strategic perspectives	Description
Analytical	Reasoning based on analytical procedures
Business model	Holistic conceptualization of the business model
Institutional	Reasoning based on social and cultural influences

Analytical Perspective

This strategic perspective is related to the analytical logic present in strategic reasoning and procedures. The literature on business strategy is full of examples of how managers make use of analytical logic, traditionally considered a cornerstone of strategic development. This logic includes, for instance, *deduction*,[5] *induction*,[6] *prediction*,[7] *causation*,[8] *and effectuation logic*.[9] By using and combining different analytical logic, strategists can evaluate alternatives, variables, indicators, and objectives in order to establish a course of action toward their desired results.

In the example we used at the beginning of this chapter, analytical logic represented the approach of the consultant, "following numbers and market estimations." Through analytical logic, strategists gain a better understanding of situations to obtain further explanations and conclusions.[10] Based on this idea, analytical perspective represents the use of procedures strategists employ as resources for understanding reality. As analytical logic is based on explicit information, it uses empirical evidence and predictions to reach conclusions. In other words, the analytical perspective reflects how strategists make use of different tools, techniques, and frameworks to make strategic choices.

Business Model Perspective

This perspective is based on the logic that allows us to conceptualize business models, initially identified as the *dominant logic*.[11] Dominant logic is the conceptualization of the business model stored as a shared cognitive map—or a set of schemas—among the dominant coalition (board of directors, management team). In other words, it is the understanding of how the business works in a particular company. It acts as a filter and enables us to process large amounts of information[12] and manage complex strategic issues.[13] The concept of dominant logic, initially identified as something unfinished and highly plastic,[14] later expanded its scope to encompass specific dimensions of value creation. These are, for example, *value creation logic*,[15] *service logic innovation*,[16] the *logic of organizational boundaries*,[17] and the *logic of exchange*.[18]

Business model logic is related to intuition, born of experience, and therefore it allows strategists to "see" solutions and opportunities beyond analytical data and procedures. Thus, business model logic requires a profound knowledge of reality that permits us to establish valid hypotheses regarding the fundamental aspects of a given business model. As business models reflect choices and their consequences,[19] this logic helps us to understand the key strategic choices informing the business. In the tale told at the beginning of this chapter, the logic of the CEO was grounded in business model logic ("I simply do not see it"). Confronted with particular situations, the business model perspective does not rely on data and analysis alone, but on the holistic representation of reality. We see this, for example, when managers pay attention to and interpreting the value creation of other companies, or experiment with value creation alternatives, or simply look beyond their existing industry and geographical borders.

Institutional Perspective

This perspective comes from the intersection of the literature on strategic management and institutionalism. Institutional logic represents the role of contingent sets of social norms and principles that shape individual and organizational behavior in the search for appropriateness.[20] "As people go through their lives, they are constantly working with, for and against multiple forms of institutional logic that shape their social and cultural contexts."[21] In other words, they represent the way society and business influence thinking inside the organization. There are several forms of institutional logic seen in business today such as: *commercial logic*,[22] *financial logic*,[23] *social welfare logic*,[24] *environmental logic*,[25] *or family logic*.[26] They shape the practice in firms when they are represented in the organization by individuals who have a cognitive and motivational affinity for them.[27] These individuals become "carriers" of institutional logic.[28] For example, salespersons can be carriers of commercial logic, controllers can be carriers of the financial logic, HR executives can be carriers of social welfare logic, and board family members can be carriers of the family logic.

In the story at the beginning of this chapter, the president's reasoning represents the institutional perspective ("we are a family-owned company, not a public company that looks only to maximizing profits"). Under this logic, strategists base their choices on the identity of the organization relative to what is legitimate and appropriate. The institutional logic helps managers to identify the right principles of the company and to recognize when they should evolve. The articulation of institutional logic into strategy can be developed through narratives, and other symbolic means, in ways that allow companies to manage the degree to which institutional logic becomes both accessible and active.

Purpose and Profit

Multi-logic approaches can be a source of enrichment for the overall strategy. However, they can be a source of conflict as well. As we have seen in our initial story, different forms of logic can lead to a situation of paralysis, instead of helping the company move forward. The fundamental problem is not the presence of different logic, but rather the lack of a focal point helping to integrate the different perspectives.

Over decades, academics have suggested that profit maximization is the overarching principle informing our logic of strategy. Under this theoretical view, analytical logic should serve the strategies that lead to profit maximization. Business model logic should aim to maximize economic value and institutional logic should be managed in such a way that allows organizations to obtain the maximum profit possible from their institutional environment.

But reality is quite distant from this. We can compare this with what, for centuries, was a wrong but somehow useful theory of the universe: the geocentric view of the cosmos. In ancient times, people believed that the earth was the center of the universe and the sun and all the stars revolved around it. Despite this being wrong, it was still a "somehow useful" explanation that helped to establish calendar calculations and astronomical charts for over 1500 years. Discordant heliocentric voices like that of Aristarco de Samos in the second century were not given much attention. Against those who challenged the heliocentric view, both moral and religious arguments were used (e.g. as with the excommunication of Galileo). The reason why geocentric views prevailed for centuries is that heliocentric predictions were not better, as a practical matter, than geocentric ones. It was not until the universal gravitation theory of Newton that the heliocentric theory definitely triumphed over the geocentric one. From then on, the geocentric theory became a "no longer useful" theory.

Something similar is happening with the view that profit maximization should be the only consideration for businesses. Despite being distant from reality—as we have known for more than 40 years[29]—this view has prevailed for decades because alternative theories did not provide better estimations (e.g. contradicting research on Corporate Social Responsibility (CSR) and performance[30]). Many purpose-driven leaders have strongly contested the profit maximization theorists with purpose-driven theories—for example, David Packard, 1960[31]—but their proposals were not given much attention in strategic theory. Purpose-driven theories were contested with categorical arguments—for example, by Milton Friedman.[32] It was not until prosocial motivation theories were accepted—demonstrating that individuals and organizations have social motivations beyond maximizing profits—that purpose-driven theories started to be accepted.[33]

This process has been accelerated by the dramatic 2008 financial crisis that helped us to recognize that the wrong but "somehow useful" theory of profit maximization was no longer useful, but actually harmful. Consider, for example, the conclusion of researchers on how Sephora, Four Seasons, and Danone US quickly recovered from the decline in profits they endured at the beginning of the financial crisis. How did they do it? Instead of focusing on one goal only, such as profits, their employees collaborated to shape a collective purpose, "that superseded individual goals and accounted for the key elements required to achieve and sustain excellence."[34] Another example is the case of the Swedish bank Handelsbanken that enjoyed continuous growth in profitability during the financial crisis. With no emphasis on maximizing returns but, instead, with a customer-centric purpose, "the goals were simply to track a moving target by always having higher customer satisfaction and profitability than a weighted average of the competition."[35] These examples, and many others, show that purpose does not mean giving up striving for excellent economic results. It requires combining purpose and profit.

We can see this, for example, in the main strategic handbooks, where the latest editions have reviewed the profit maximization dogmas elucidated in earlier editions.[36] Or in the vast majority of the new frameworks for strategy—for example, blue ocean, lean, agile—where purpose is placed at the very core of strategy. We believe Larry Fink, the CEO of BlackRock, the largest investment firm in the world, set the example when he demanded companies in which his firm invests to embrace a social purpose, stating: "every company must not only deliver financial performance, but also show how it makes a positive contribution to society."[37] This reflects a growing awareness of our current reality. Purpose is not only the result of psychological forces but also, and with the same intensity, the result of social and economic pressures.

Coupling Strategy with Purpose

Since Bartlett and Ghoshal first made their proposal in 1993 to shift from strategy to purpose,[38] many strategists have been won over to the idea. As we see it, the fundamental question is not choosing between purpose and strategy but instead putting *purpose at the center of strategy*. In this sense, we believe purpose should be infused with multi-logic strategy and vice versa. While purpose should not be considered a strategy, purpose requires strategy.

Every strategic logic we have seen provides a fundamental contribution to the development of purpose in the organization. The various forms of strategic logic contribute to purpose development in the following areas: analytical coupling, business model coupling, and institutional coupling.

Analytical coupling is related to the way purpose become concrete in plans and objectives that express the dynamism of purpose in practice. In this vein, purpose plays the role of an overarching *constraint* that helps managers maintain a firm focus on purpose, while concentrating their efforts on activities such as strategic analysis, planning, and implementation. One illustration of this can be seen in Google. The dexterity Google exhibits in big data and analytical tools helps them decide which products move forward and which are discontinued. This is in direct relation to the company's purpose, which is to "organize the world's information and make it universally accessible and useful." This coupling between analytical logic and purpose can be developed by different means. There is, for example, the practice of putting the purpose at the very beginning of any strategic initiative, or using purpose-driven indicators to evaluate how well the organization is fulfilling its purpose.

Business model coupling regards the way value creation strategies and business models are conceptualized under the framework of purpose. By imbedding purpose in business models, it helps purpose sustainability, eliminating potential conflicts between purpose and profit. This is the approach, for example, of *shared value*, the concept that calls companies to establish their business model around the intersection of business interests and social needs.[39] This is also referred to as "massive transformative purpose," a common trait found in the fastest growing startups of the world like TED or Singularity University.[40] From this perspective, purpose is not only a constraint but also a source of *opportunity*. Such is the case for IKEA, a pioneer in configuring its business model consistent to its purpose of "creating a better everyday life for the many." The coupling between purpose and business models can be reinforced by practices such as

Table 4.2 The three strategic perspectives integrated with purpose

Perspectives	Purpose as	Examples
Analytical	Constraint	Purpose as a filter for strategic decision-making Purpose-driven indicators
Business model	Opportunity	Shared valueBrand purpose
Institutional	Legitimacy	Institutional framing Stakeholder management

purpose-driven innovation or brand purpose, which help businesses to evolve and reconfigure themselves around the fulfillment of purpose.

Institutional coupling is related to the way organizations develop institutional principles and values with regard to organizational purpose. It offers companies the ability to both maintain equilibrium between the company and its stakeholders as well as provide organizational members a source of higher meaning and motivation. We see a great example of this in Johnson & Johnson's credo, which has served the company for decades as a beacon by establishing its relationship between stakeholders and company members. By connecting purpose and institutional logic, strategists tap into a deeper source of motivation, as "one of the most effective ways to influence behavior is to influence [a person's] identification with a given logic and its associated practices."[41] In this regard, purpose acts as a source of *legitimacy*, guiding strategy by the primary principle of acting accordingly to "who you are." This can be promoted by practices such as institutional framing (missions, values, principles) or stakeholder management, where a company preserves purpose through the evolution and reconfiguration of its institutional environment (Table 4.2).

Integrating of the Three Perspectives

Beyond the specific contribution of each perspective, their highest potential comes by combining the three forms of logic with purpose simultaneously. Take for example the cases of Google, IKEA, and Johnson & Johnson, they demonstrate that success does not come from one perspective of logic alone, but from integrating purpose with all three. In the case of Google, analytical dexterity shows an outstanding fit between purpose and business model innovation, while also winning admiration and legitimacy in social arenas. Consider also the lessons that Yoffie and Cusumano derived from the study of Steve Jobs, Bill Gates, and Andy Grove.[42] The way in which their strategies were built is a good illustration of how the three forms of logic guide their decisions (e.g. dexterity in analysis, synthesis of information, big picture vision, and using guiding principles to generate game-changing business models).

This approach is consistent with literature that recognizes the multiplicity of logic as a source of strategic heterogeneity and innovation that help strategists develop more consistent purpose-driven strategies.[43] In this view, beyond the salient logic related to individual characteristics, such as an individual's role in the organization, motivational affinity, or institutional biography,[44] purpose-driven strategies call for the combination of each perspective in a harmonious way. From a practical perspective, integrating each logic with purpose can be done by using what we call *integrated tools*. These are combinations of existing models—for example, SWOT analysis, Porter's five forces, business model canvas, balanced scorecard—that form new tools and stimulate the integration of each strategic perspective with purpose.[45]

An example of this and a very powerful tool is the *Purpose Model Canvas*. It is an integrated tool that we have used with much success in companies of different sectors and sizes, ranging from big multinational corporations to local medium-sized companies. The tool is based on a model developed by Casadesus-Ricart.[46] This model, extensively explained in previous publications,[47] links choices and consequences by arrows based on causality theories, enabling users to identify virtuous cycles—feedback loops that strengthen the business model at every iteration. Based on this, the purpose model canvas helps the user contemplate all strategic choices and consequences forming the business model (e.g. pricing, segmentation, cost efficiency, productivity, marketing, customer service, innovation, recruitment). Then it considers the institutional principles of the company—its values, missions, policies, fundamental beliefs.

Once it has identified the key institutional and business model choices and their consequences, the user can identify whether a company's strategy is coherent enough to enhance purpose fulfillment in these four areas:

Alignment: refers to choices delivering consequences that move the organization toward fulfilling its stated purpose in that it helps to clarify which decisions fit (and which do not) into the organization's purpose.

Reinforcement: refers to choices that complement each other in the fulfillment of purpose. It takes the best from the existing capabilities to create synergies that amplify the impact of purpose.

Virtuousness: refers to virtuous circles, the feedback loops between choices and consequences, that help purpose to gain strength over time. Virtuousness is like the internal engine of purpose. It pushes purpose forward in every interaction and is the key distinguisher between great and mediocre purpose impact.

Sustainability: refers to the ability to sustain purpose fulfillment over time. It considers the challenges facing purpose that come from the competitive capacities of the business itself (e.g. imitation, substitution) or from the institutional environment (e.g., social shifts, reputation).

Finally, for each criterion, the model deploys analytical logic through indicators that evaluate various key aspects of the model (e.g. reinforcements between choices or virtuous circles). These indicators help to assess both how a company fulfills its purpose as well as the elements that fuel its fulfillment. In sum, the purpose model canvas helps us to see the connection between the "what," the "how," and the "why."

Figure 4.1 shows a simplified and basic example of the purpose model canvas, illustrating the reinforcement of each perspective. First, the business model is depicted by the company's key virtuous cycle (high volume, economies of scale, low cost, lost value) the key elements that reinforce it (low price reputation, supplier loyalty) and the overall result (high margins). Second, it shows how the institutional principles—environmental awareness, culture of service and cost consciousness—strengthen the virtuous cycle. Finally, it displays the key indicators (customer survey, gross yield per employee) that monitor alignment, reinforcement, virtuousness, and robustness of the whole model.

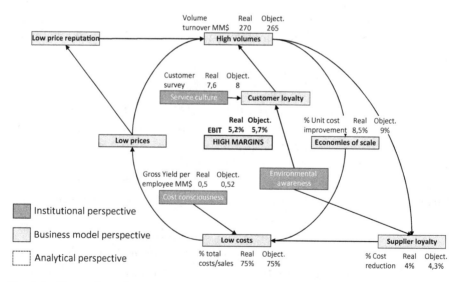

Fig. 4.1 Illustration of a "purpose model canvas"

By using the purpose model canvas, we have seen how companies fuel strategy, reinforcing inspiration with analytical rigor over time. Indeed, this is the strategy we think best fits the example presented at the beginning of the chapter. More than simply coupling the logic of the consultant, president, and CEO with purpose, a purpose-driven strategy calls for jointly integrating each perspective with purpose, helping to establish a harmonious way forward.

Notes

1. Paroutis, S., & Heracleous, L. (2013). Discourse revisited: Dimensions and employment of first-order strategy discourse during institutional adoption. *Strategic Management Journal, 34*(8), 935–956.
2. Sandberg, J., & Tsoukas, H. (2011). Grasping the logic of practice: Theorizing through practical rationality. *Academy of Management Review, 36*(2), 338–360.
3. Greenwood, R., Raynard, M., Kodeih, F., Micelotta, E. R., & Lounsbury, M. (2011). Institutional complexity and organizational responses. *Academy of Management Annals, 5*(1), 317–371.
4. Paroutis, S., & Heracleous, L. (2013). Discourse revisited: Dimensions and employment of first-order strategy discourse during institutional adoption. *Strategic Management Journal, 34*(8), 935–956.
5. Deduction logic: Reasoning that determines the validity of the conclusion if the premise of the rule is observed to be true. Dong, A., Garbuio, M., & Lovallo, D. (2016). Generative sensing. *California Management Review, 58*(4), 97–117.
6. Induction logic: Reasoning based on a limited set of cases to establish a degree of empirical truth for a hypothesis. Ibidem.
7. Prediction logic: Takes the environment as outside the control of the decision-maker, who therefore attempts to predict and adapt to changes in it. Read, S., Dew, N., Sarasvathy, S. D., Song, M., & Wiltbank, R. (2009). Marketing under uncertainty: The logic of an effectual approach. *Journal of Marketing, 73*(3), 1–18.
8. Causation logic: Logical process that aims to reach a predefined goal. Sarasvathy, S. D. (2001). Causation and effectuation: Toward a theoretical shift from economic inevitability to entrepreneurial contingency. *Academy of Management Review, 26*(2), 243–263.
9. Effectuation logic: An inversion of predictive rationality in the creation of new firms, products, services, and markets. Ibidem.
10. Nadkarni, S., & Barr, P. S. (2008). Environmental context, managerial cognition, and strategic action: An integrated view. *Strategic Management Journal, 29*(13), 1395–1427.

11. Bettis, R. A., & Prahalad, C. K. (1995). The dominant logic: Retrospective and extension. *Strategic Management Journal, 16*(1), 5–14.

12. Reger, R. K., & Huff, A. S. (1993). Strategic groups: A cognitive perspective. *Strategic Management Journal, 14*(2), 103–123.

13. Lampel, J., & Shamsie, J. (2000). Probing the unobtrusive link: Dominant logic and the design of joint ventures at General Electric. *Strategic Management Journal, 21*, 593–602.

14. Von Krogh, G., & Roos, J. (1996). A tale of the unfinished. *Strategic Management Journal, 17*, 729–737.

15. Value creation logic: Describes the focus and means to create value-adding services. Möller, K., Rajala, R., & Westerlund, M. (2008). Service innovation myopia? A new recipe for client-provider value creation. *California Management Review, 50*(3), 31–48.

16. Service logic innovation: Conceptualization of the customer (user, buyer, and payer) and the related service innovation. Michel, S., Brown, S. W., & Gallan, A. S. (2008). Service-logic innovations: How to innovate customers, not products. *California Management Review, 50*(3), 49–65.

17. Logic of organizational boundaries: Related to organizational boundaries regarding efficiency, power, competence, and identity. Santos, F. M., & Eisenhardt, K. M. (2005). Organizational boundaries and theories of organization. *Organization Science, 16*(5), 491–508.

18. Logic of exchange: Conceptualization of value in an exchange relationship. McGinn, K. L., & Keros, A. T. (2002). Improvisation and the logic of exchange in socially embedded transactions. *Administrative Science Quarterly, 47*(3), 442–473.

19. Casadesus-Masanell, R., & Ricart, J. E. (2010). From strategy to business models and onto tactics. *Long Range Planning, 43*(2), 195–215.

20. Vurro, C., Dacin, M. T., & Perrini, F. (2010). Institutional antecedents of partnering for social change: How institutional logics shape cross-sector social partnerships. *Journal of Business Ethics, 94*, 39–53.

21. Bertels, S., & Lawrence, T. B. (2016). Organizational responses to institutional complexity stemming from emerging logics: The role of individuals. *Strategic Organization, 14*(4), 336–372.

22. Commercial logic: Structured around selling products and services in the market to produce an economic surplus. Venkataraman, H., Vermeulen, P., Raaijmakers, A., & Mair, J. (2016). Market meets community: Institutional logics as strategic resources for development work. *Organization Studies, 37*(5), 709–733.

23. Financial logic: Characterized in terms of profit-maximizing objectives and self-interest. Almandoz, J. (2012). Arriving at the starting line: The impact of community and financial logics on new banking ventures. *Academy of Management Journal, 55*(6), 1381–1406.

24. Social welfare logic: Structured around a predominant goal: Making products and services available to address local social needs. Pache, A. C., & Santos, F. (2013). Inside the hybrid organization: Selective coupling as a response to competing institutional logics. *Academy of Management Journal, 56*(4), 972–1001.

25. Environmental logic: Concerned with protecting the natural environment and decreasing the firm's impact on natural resources. Dahlmann, F., & Grosvold, J. (2017). Environmental managers and institutional work: Reconciling tensions of competing institutional logics. *Business Ethics Quarterly, 27*(2), 263–291.

26. Family logic: Concerned with providing stability and secure income to family members. Belenzon, S., Patacconi, A., & Zarutskie, R. (2016). Married to the firm? A large-scale investigation of the social context of ownership. *Strategic Management Journal, 37*(13), 2611–2638.

27. Pache, A. C., & Santos, F. (2010). When worlds collide: The internal dynamics of organizational responses to conflicting institutional demands. *Academy of Management Review, 35*(3), 455–476.

28. Almandoz, J. (2014). Founding teams as carriers of competing logics: When institutional forces predict banks' risk exposure. *Administrative Science Quarterly, 59*(3), 442–473.

29. Koplin, H. T. (1963). The profit maximization assumption. *Oxford Economic Papers, 15*(2), 130–139.

30. McWilliams, A., & Siegel, D. (2000). Corporate social responsibility and financial performance: Correlation or misspecification?. *Strategic Management Journal, 21*(5), 603–609.

31. Collins, J. C., & Porras, J. I. (1996). Building your company's vision. *Harvard Business Review, 74*(5), 65.

32. "There is one and only one social responsibility of business: to use its resources and engage in activities designed to increase its profits so long as it stays within the rules of the game, which is to say, engages in open and free competition without deception or fraud." Friedman, M. (1962). *Capitalism and freedom*. Chicago: University of Chicago Press.

33. For example, Parmar et al. demonstrate simultaneously an increase in self-determination for a corporate objective focused on stakeholders and a decrease in self-determination for a corporate objective focused on profits and shareholders. Parmar, B. L., Keevil, A., & Wicks, A. C. (2019). People and profits: The impact of corporate objectives on employees' need satisfaction at work. *Journal of Business Ethics, 154*(1), 13.

34. Ready, D. A., & Truelove, E. (2011). The power of collective ambition. *Harvard Business Review*.

35. Birkinshaw, J., Foss, N. J., & Lindenberg, S. (2014). Combining purpose with profits. *MIT Sloan Management Review, 55*(3), 49.

36. Grant, R. M. (2016). *Contemporary strategy analysis*. Hoboken, NJ: John Wiley & Sons.

37. https://www.blackrock.com/corporate/investor-relations/larry-fink-ceo-letter

38. Bartlett, C. A., & Ghoshal, S. (1993). Beyond the M-form: Toward a managerial theory of the firm. *Strategic Management Journal, 14*(S2), 23–46.

39. Porter, M. E., & Kramer, M. R. (2011). The big idea: Creating shared value. How to reinvent capitalism—And unleash a wave of innovation and growth. *Harvard Business Review, 89*(1–2).

40. Ismail, S. (2014). *Exponential organizations: Why new organizations are ten times better, faster, and cheaper than yours (and what to do about it)*. New York: Diversion Books.

41. Lok, J. (2010). Institutional logics as identity projects. *Academy of Management Journal, 53*(6), 1305–1335.

42. Yoffie, D. B., & Cusumano, M. A. (2015). *Strategy rules: Five timeless lessons from Bill Gates, Andy Grove, and Steve Jobs*. New York: Harper Business.

43. Ocasio, W., & Radoynovska, N. (2016). Strategy and commitments to institutional logics: Organizational heterogeneity in business models and governance. *Strategic Organization, 14*(4), 287–309.

44. Martin, G., Currie, G., Weaver, S., Finn, R., & McDonald, R. (2017). Institutional complexity and individual responses: Delineating the boundaries of partial autonomy. *Organization Studies, 38*(1), 103–127.

45. Ricart, J. E., & Rey, C. (2017, March–April). Strategising for the future. *The European Business Review*, 7–11.

46. Casadesus-Masanell, R., & Ricart, J. E. (2011, January). How to design a winning business model. *Harvard Business Review*, pp. 100–107.

47. Casadesus-Masanell, R., & Ricart, J. E. (2010). From strategy to business models and onto tactics. *Long Range Planning, 43*(2), 195–215.

5

Purpose-driven Leadership

Pablo Cardona, Carlos Rey, and Nick Craig

"No man can live the dream of another man." With these words, Jeff Gravenhorst, the CEO of the Danish multinational ISS Facility Services initiated a worldwide program called "find your apple." Its aim was to create a sense of purpose among its more than 500,000 employees. Through this initiative, the company regularly invites employees to gather into small groups, where members of its maintenance, cleaning, and catering services—with the aid of trained colleagues—help each other reflect on their raison d'être and the purpose of their work. In creating a purpose-driven company, Jeff didn't make a speech about purpose. Instead, he let purpose speak for itself.[1]

Today, an increasing number of successful companies around the world are experiencing a major change in the way they understand leadership. From the traditional single leader at the top model, they are moving into a paradigm

P. Cardona (✉)
School of Management and Communication, Universidad Internacional de La Rioja, La Rioja, Spain
e-mail: pablo.cardona@unir.net

C. Rey
Universitat Internacional de Catalunya,
Barcelona, Spain
e-mail: carlosrey@uic.es

N. Craig
Core Leadership Institute, Harvard, USA
e-mail: ncraig@coreleader.com

© The Author(s) 2019
C. Rey et al. (eds.), *Purpose-driven Organizations*,
https://doi.org/10.1007/978-3-030-17674-7_5

57

whereby leadership is distributed throughout the entirety of the firm. The reason is simple: in this new, ever-changing world, we need not only colleagues' head, we also need their heart. In other words, rather than leaders surrounded by followers, the new environment demands leaders surrounded by leaders, a phenomenon that researchers describe as *shared leadership*. Shared leadership is a system of mutually influential interactions in groups at different levels with the aim of achieving a collective goal.[2] Though shared leadership may be based on various elements, in this chapter, we focus on a form of shared leadership that is based on the idea of shared purpose, which we refer to as *Purpose-driven Leadership* (PDL).

In the traditional leadership paradigm, "communicating purpose is the most central of all leadership behaviors."[3] As such, purpose should be developed at the upper echelons of the company—often with the assistance of a consulting firm—and then communicated downward throughout the company. The goal of this communication is to align the whole of the organization around a predefined purpose. While alignment has been considered the key to attaining extraordinary performance in the past, new studies are finding that it may no longer be the right approach to succeed in the creation of a common purpose.[4]

Shared purpose cannot simply be invented at the top—only to be imposed downward. The reality is, purpose already exists and is alive.[5] This is the paradigm shift and it challenges our traditional understanding of leadership. In that, it is not merely about communicating the firm's purpose but rather discovering (and rediscovering) the shared purpose that already exists within the company. In the PDL paradigm, influence is not in the hands of one or a few, but in the hands of all who share the purpose and thus are eager to make it come to life in their work. These actions cannot be taken solely by the group leader, but must be taken by the group as a whole. The result is not just a relative level of employee alignment, but an authentic commitment by each employee to fulfill his or her responsibilities with a sense of honor and obligation that only arises from a fully internalized understanding of the shared purpose.

In an organization run by PDL, living examples are more powerful than communication. Or, should we say, giving example is the only valid way to communicate. And along with this, other leadership skills become increasingly important. For example, shared leadership research has found that leaders who value and respect the purpose of their collaborators and colleagues as much as they value and respect their own are more effective.[6] Further, leaders who are willing to support those in the development of their purpose receive more help in return. Finally, leaders who base their relationships on trust, freedom, and respect develop stronger bonds of shared leadership. And this transformation happens more naturally than one would think, as all human beings essentially have a calling to act as leaders. It is not just an option; humans need leadership for personal fulfillment and to reach their full potential. Purpose-driven leadership releases a greater potential of human capacity, helping individuals reach higher satisfaction and meaning at work.

However, in order to better understand the new challenges of PDL, we need to review briefly the underlying approach of the traditional leadership models.

Traditional Leadership Models

Leadership has been studied during the twentieth century under different aspects, as a subject for sociology, politics, psychology, pedagogy, ethics, and business. These studies have mostly focused on the person at the top of the group, organization, or society. Theories developed in the first half of the twentieth century looked at the distinctive innate qualities that were common in great social and political leaders, such as Lincoln or Gandhi. However, in 1948, research analyzed many of these studies and concluded that there was no combination of traits that consistently differentiated leaders from non-leaders in different situations.[7] In fact, we have seen a person can be a good leader in one situation and a bad one in another.

In the 1960s, the analysis moved from qualities to actions, and focused on how leaders should behave in different situations. One of the best-known models from that time was the situational leadership framework.[8] In this model, different management styles are more effective for specific subordinate types. The subordinates were then classified into four categories, from lowest to highest maturity, depending on their levels of competence and motivation.

Starting in the seventies, studies of leadership focused more on the relationship between leaders and subordinates. One of the first studies with this focus was the Leader-Member Exchange.[9] According to this theory, leaders build high/low quality exchange relationships with their subordinates, depending on the level of trust, respect, and obligation between the manager and each subordinate. Later, leadership was defined more specifically as a *relationship of influence* between the leader and his or her followers (now called collaborators).[10] Out of this set of theories, two main schools have dominated the field of leadership studies in the last decades: transformational and servant leadership.

During the nineties, transformational leadership was embodied in a type of leader with great energy for change and the ability to manage large organizations. The essence of the transformational leader was characterized by a radically new *vision*: he or she possessed an image of an achievable future that improved upon the present situation and proved appealing to his or her followers. Transformational leaders are characterized by extraordinary will, and distinguish themselves by four main characteristics: charisma, inspirational motivation, intellectual stimulation, and individualized consideration.[11]

Transformational leadership could be found, for example, in the case of GE under the Jack Welch tenure. "Revered widely as a charismatic and exemplary CEO," Welch was fawned upon by media commentators as the best CEO of his generation, depicted glowingly in several hagiographies as a master transformer of a business. His leadership style was admired and emulated by many "as pedagogue, physician, architect, commander and saint."[12] Mainly due to its popularity and proven effectiveness in moments of change, transformational leadership is still one of the main models taught in training courses and business schools.

The second approach, called servant leadership, "originates from the natural feeling of wanting to serve, to primarily serve. Only then the conscious decision appears to aspire to lead."[13] The essence of the servant leader is characterized by a radical mission: a commitment to "serving others." In this regard, the influence of servant leadership is deeper than that of transformational leaders, as it appeals to the need for people to find meaning in their work. Servant leaders are rooted in humility—extraordinary modesty—as these leaders put themselves and their vision in the service of a higher purpose. A plethora of anecdotal evidence has been used in the past to show examples of the servant leadership approach. Think for example on Jack Lowe, CEO between 1980 and 2004 of TD Industries, a US-based mechanical contractor ranked as one of the best companies to work for by the *Fortune* magazine. Based on a "servant leadership philosophy as the foundation of trusting relationships in the organization," he established outstanding levels of trust and was able to make radical changes in the organization.[14]

These two perspectives—transformational and servant—are not mutually exclusive. In fact, they necessarily complement each other. When transformational leaders forget the social character of the organizational purpose, leadership becomes an act of self-aggrandizement, the seeking of personal glory. Some authors call this the narcissistic leader.[15] On the other hand, leadership without a challenging vision will eventually turn into a bureaucratic form of paternalism, which at an organizational level leads to inertia and stagnation.

These corruptions of leadership can only be avoided by a careful balance of transformational and servant leadership, in a positive combination of influence styles. In fact, some studies show that leaders in companies with the highest growth present a pattern of leadership characterized by both extraordinary will and humility, skills that combine the two schools. Such leaders show a combination of "compelling modesty" and "unwavering resolve."[16]

Challenging the Hierarchical Leadership

The traditional leadership models have a common characteristic: they are all *hierarchical*. These models understand leadership as a top-down process from those with more formal power (i.e., the managers) to those with less formal power (i.e., the employees). Through decades of development, employees have been granted a more proactive role in this process, evolving from mere subordinates, to followers, and finally, to collaborators. The results are clear: the more proactive employees can become, the better is the resulting performance.[17] However, the dynamic is essentially the same: only the person in the highest position of the hierarchy can exercise leadership. Even in the case of empowering leaders, that is, leaders who share some aspects of the decision-making power, leadership is a privilege reserved only to the top position in the relationship.

In a business world characterized by accelerated transformation, the trend of leaders becoming less authoritarian and collaborators becoming more proactive is self-evident. The traditional idea of a leader at the top—or any position in the middle—is that of the one who knows best where and how to react to the changes in the market. This now, at the very least, is controversial. But the hierarchical model resists, and leaders remain attached to hierarchical power, even at the expense of losing leadership potential in the organization. Mainstream research keeps digging in the same direction: revisiting the benefits of empowerment, proactivity, and employee voice, without solving the structural problem that results from confining the leadership role to a single person in power.

However, the association between leadership and hierarchy is a self-imposed limitation on the essence of leadership as an influence relationship. Leadership can be exercised top-down, laterally, and/or bottom-up, as long as people involved in the relationship accept their role and responsibilities. Besides, sharing leadership does not necessarily damage the benefits of a hierarchical structure. Indeed, hierarchies have a managerial and controlling function that does not overlap with the leadership process. Hierarchies are in place wherever there is a need to exercise power. But leadership is not about power. In fact, power-based leadership only produces poor leadership results, such as in the case of transactional leadership. PDL, a deep relationship of mutual influence that creates a real sense of purpose, is based on trust. And trust does not require any particular position of power. Even those in a position of power need to exercise their power in a way that does not destroy trust because managers cannot force true commitment using their power, but only by engaging in trustworthy behaviors.[18]

The main problem is: how do we create co-leadership dynamics within an organizational structure? Although shared leadership processes have been studied for a long time, they usually operate in contexts that lack hierarchical structures, like in the case of self-managed teams.[19] The results of these studies show some advantage to shared leadership as compared to hierarchical leadership in areas such as task satisfaction, but generally fail to deliver better performance results. As a result, shared leadership still remains largely in the sphere of managerial theories, especially in the area of team dynamics, rather than being applied in real world cases. As leadership researchers have recently revealed, "Despite the widespread attention given to the importance of shared purpose, it is the rare leader who successfully establishes it."[20]

The Rise of Purpose-driven Leadership

Traditional leadership theories and training courses focus on "What" leaders do and "How" they do it. New leaders want to learn from examples of successful leaders as to how to become leaders themselves: how to make tough decisions, how to create a transformational vision, how to develop loyal followers, and so on. They treat leadership as a competency, where behaviors or skills can be learned, or even worse, as a technique that can be replicated. However, purpose-driven leadership is much more focused on the "why" and the purpose. Rather than looking at what leaders do, PDL is more interested in understanding why leaders do what they do.

Think about Mandela, Gandhi, Lincoln, Muhammad, or Jesus Christ. The very essence of their leadership is not in "what" that they did, but "why" they did it. And this is something that cannot be imitated, because the "why" is exclusive and specific to every individual. Every purpose-driven leader has a unique "why" that makes each leader different from any other leader. Personal purpose encompasses life's meaning and indicates what one lives for, his or her deepest aspirations. Personal purpose is unique to every individual, and only

Table 5.1 Fundamentals of purpose-driven leadership (PDL)

Purpose-driven leadership
Discovering your personal purpose
Helping others find their personal purpose
Connecting personal to organizational purpose

he, or she, determines the real meaning and relevance of a personal purpose. It indicates what that person stands for, what makes that person unique. Thus, the development of a purpose-driven leader does not consist of acquiring a list of competencies and techniques to become as similar as possible to the role model leaders of the moment. Rather, it is the process of personal development and the discovery of purpose that will make the leader's life truly authentic and meaningful. Because of this, in PDL, every leader is different and must be different.

In fact, having worked with thousands of leaders from around the world, Nick Craig of the Core Leadership Institute has never found two to be the same. Beyond and beneath the standard and superficial "save the world" aspirations are the powerful and unique gifts of purpose. These purpose statements give the flavor of just *how* unique:

I am the LEGO poet who builds a bridge from head to heart (Max, senior HR executive).
Input = $\int$Data $*$ People @me (Rikkya, senior finance executive).
I come, I learn, I fix (Jeff, software development executive).

Based on our research and experience, the essence of PDL is based on three undertakings: first, the discovery of personal purpose; second, helping others find their personal purpose; and finally, connecting personal to organizational purpose (see Table 5.1). These three are the same at all levels of the company. It is not a linear model, neither is it top-down, horizontal, nor bottom-up. It is concentric and acts in all directions.

Discovering Your Leadership Purpose

A leader, before leading others, leads himself. Often PDL is presented as if the leader were naturally and irrevocably connected to his personal purpose, as if purpose-driven leaders were born with their purpose imprinted. But nothing could be further from the truth. Personal purpose is developed through great efforts, forged through an interior dialogue, by leaders who are determined to keep their personal purpose in their memory and reflected in their actions. And this is done constantly, every day. Through personal purpose, leaders find energy to influence those around them. This question, that many companies are increasingly discovering, is fundamental to understanding purpose-driven leadership and the dynamics that allow its expansion throughout organizations. It is what some call "leading from purpose."[21]

The "discovery" of purpose has two implications. The first one is related to understanding your personal purpose. Individuals must ask themselves *why* they want to become leaders, *why* they want to influence others.[22] Leadership purpose springs from one's identity, "the essence of who you are."[23]

For many leaders, this identity lies in key childhood experiences. Ranjay, a senior HR executive, knew that his earliest memories were of being on stage. He loved being in the spotlight, performing alone or as a cast member. If he did not have a script he liked, he would write one. Example after example throughout his life re-enforced a common thread that clarified his purpose, "Bring people to center stage, Lights! Camera! Action!" Once he realized this, his career and personal life made sense in a way they had not before. He knew now who he was and what he brought to a meeting or moment that was his unique gift.

Some characteristics of leadership purpose are as follows:

- It is related to the past, present, and future of who you are and who you want to be.
- It captures the unique gift you bring to the world. Ask, if someone with the same skills you have were to do the same job you do, what would be different? What would be different in your company if you were not working there?
- It is related to your inner motivations and values.
- It is not invented or chosen on an ad hoc basis, but is encountered or found from within (sometimes by trial and error).
- When you are connected with that purpose, it provides focus and energy.
- It affects all parts of your life. In work, family, friends, and social activities. Purpose can have different manifestations, but the essence remains the same.

The second implication is about rediscovering the purpose in everything you do, is about the capacity to recognize purpose in the daily activities and interactions with others.[24] In this sense, personal purpose is not a destination but a "path." Purpose gives meaning, but does not replace the personal effort of finding meaning in daily matters. Purpose must be always surprising, always new, and always present. Purpose is what makes every person different from others, and at the same time, it makes every day different from all others.

Discovering and rediscovering personal purpose is a completely different approach to traditional leadership and, in our experience, it is much more effective. For every person needs to understand the unique gift they bring to the world. It is the natural way individuals encounter their leadership potential.

Helping Others to Discover Their Leadership Purpose

Purpose-driven organizations are full of intimate relationships developed around purpose because purpose is entirely personal but not solitary. It is a "path" that co-creates with the purpose of others. It is a personal voyage ingrained in a collective journey. Think of a sailor who travels in a boat with a crew and a direction. His purpose cannot be disconnected from the purpose of his crew. Purpose is not a lonely, self-referential point but rather has impact and transcends the purpose of others.

This reality can be seen in many of the great leaders studied throughout history. These leaders received help from others to discover and rediscover their own personal purpose and, at the same time, they helped others to discover and rediscover their purpose. One person can do this even with a very small number of people, but its effect multiplies as leaders implicitly show others how to do the same with the other people they have in their sphere of influence. It is like a drop of water on a lake that ripples ever outward.

Helping others to discover their purpose includes sharing your own purpose while at the same time "listening" and embracing the purpose of others. It goes in a bidirectional way. It means helping others and receiving help from others. Sharing your personal purpose will be necessary for the discovery of purpose as "you can't get a clear picture of yourself without trusted colleagues or friends to act as mirrors."[25] It keeps the flame of purpose alive and glowing even brighter. When you share your purpose with others, it extends a commitment to your own purpose as well as helping others discover theirs.

Helping others to discover their purpose means not only caring about "what" others do but also about "why" they do what they do. It is about embracing and accepting diversity. And of course, everyone must be conscious that it is always the other person who decides how and when to share their purpose. Helping others to discover their purpose is like a dance where the other person establishes the rhythm and the tempo.

This is quite different from what is usually taught in leadership courses. This kind of influence is not based on charisma or on inspiring rhetoric. It comes from personal contact. It is a kind of leadership that takes place in an intimate way.[26] This is rarely appreciated on the outside and many times is exercised without either the leader or the person who is led realizing it. It is what some call "true leadership."[27] Exceptionally, this leadership is exercised through concrete actions (e.g., acting as a mirror to discern and reflect another's purpose), but ordinarily, and principally, this leadership is exercised by friendship and love of benevolence.[28] Because, as research has consistently demonstrated, purpose-driven leadership is always accompanied by employees' "efforts to provide emotional and psychological strength to one another."[29]

This might be surprising, but research is consistent in demonstrating that without intimate and trustworthy relationships, it is not possible to develop purpose-driven leadership.[30] Indeed, it is not by coincidence that purpose-driven organizations spend considerable amounts of resources and time with their employees in hopes of developing more meaningful relationships. While for many companies these may be simple socialization exercises, for purpose-driven companies these are seen as one of the most effective ways to expand leadership.

Connecting Personal and Organizational Purpose

The third basic fundament of PDL entails finding connections between personal and organizational purpose. As purpose is expansive (personal and organizational), its natural development is about discovering points of intersection. Purpose-driven leaders not only influence because of their personal purpose but because of the way they integrate personal purpose at work and, ultimately, connect it with the shared purpose of the organization.

At the beginning of his tenure as CEO of Ben & Jerry's, Jostein Solheim did not know what his purpose was. He was happy riding the wave of the Ben & Jerry's purpose of changing the world by creating amazing ice cream through linked prosperity for everyone connected to the business. Yet, 18 months into a 24-month turn-around assignment, the question of what he should do next pushed for an answer. Should he take a promised two-level promotion or stay at Ben & Jerry's? It was not helpful to look through the lens of the company's purpose. Jostein needed to know what was *his* journey that he needed to take and how did it fit, or not, with Ben and Jerry's.

When Jostein looked at his purpose "to thrive in paradox and ambiguity for things that really matter," it called for him to stay. He realized that if he took the promotion, other people—his staff at Ben & Jerry's—would be living his purpose. To run Ben & Jerry's with both founders still on the board while also being part of a huge multinational consumer goods company (Unilever) was the definition of paradox and ambiguity. Few would have said yes, but Jostein's purpose was perfectly designed for this adventure. When he announced that he was staying, the team that was the magic behind the brand realized that here was a guy who really believed in the purpose of Ben & Jerry's.[31]

When leaders connect their own purpose to the organizational purpose, their influence intensifies. This connection creates an effect that enhances purpose-driven leadership beyond the individual possibilities of each of its members. By these connections, leaders create a common source from which they draw leadership. Personal purpose is the essence of PDL, but it is ultimately the connection to corporate purpose that gives the individual the authority to act as a leader. This requires putting the company's purpose at the center of leadership. In this sense, organizational purpose acts as a source of authority for being THE leader within the organization. Individuals can exercise some kind of leadership based on his or her personal purpose or charisma, but that it is quite distant of what we talk here. PDL is about embracing organizational purpose from the perspective of personal purpose. PDL demands low "ego" in a context of "commitment, cooperation and openness to change", fostered by a sense of common purpose.[32]

This kind of leadership does not require a gifted person, but simply a person willing to put their gifts to the service of a collective purpose. As stated by Manuel Jimenez, CEO of a major auto parts company in the south of Spain: "in our company, the warehouse lads and distribution porters—many of them without even basic studies—understand very well what leadership is. They share a common purpose, that is what makes them leaders." This form of leadership can often be seen, for example, in top performing sports teams. In such teams, the maximum potential of leadership is not based on technical skills or knowledge, but in leadership born from common purpose. There, all members share the same purpose, and, in turn, exert continuous and sustained influence to reinforce the leadership of others. In fact, in sports teams, success or failure is often attributed to the generation of what we could call multi-influence leadership. This phenomenon has been studied by many management experts, and in recent decades there has been a growing interest in applying it to business practices.

Integrating Traditional and Purpose-driven Leadership

Discovering your personal purpose, helping others to find their personal purpose, and connecting the personal and organizational purpose are the fundamentals of purpose-driven leadership. These three undertakings offer a new perspective on leadership that enhances the traditional approaches, unveiling the leadership potential of every individual, providing authenticity and unity in leadership. To the extent that organizations combine PDL with other leadership arrangements as a compelling vision (transformation leadership), service (servant leadership), or adapting their leadership styles to the different contexts (situational leadership), they can reinforce their leadership influence and make it more inspirational and effective. Indeed, all these arrangements are necessary for organizational purpose to develop.

However, the full development of PDL requires a fundamental change in the logic of leadership. It requires overcoming the strong inertia exerted by the top-down leadership model, which is the most common model applied in organizations today. We must move away from hierarchical leadership, where only the vision of the "boss" matters, toward shared leadership, which is grounded on a combination of personal and shared purpose. Managers must learn to be "leaders of leaders," developing the leadership of others and helping them to do the same by cascading leadership throughout the entire organization. Thus, leadership, without losing its essence, must overcome the personalistic features of the hierarchical model and move on to lead purpose through a shared leadership model. In order to develop this, it will be essential for managers to overcome the idea that "they are the leaders" and others should be, and remain, their followers. Those in management positions must see others as potential leaders, not just as followers. Consequently, managers must avoid having employees merely following them by focusing their efforts on everyone, themselves included, so as to encourage every individual to pursue his or her own purpose within the context of a shared purpose. In this sense, all levels of employees must seek to change the perception of their roles, since they are no longer followers, but leaders that share a common purpose.

Notes

1. Malbašić, I., Rey, C., & Posarić, N. (2018). Congruence between personal and organizational mission: The role of balanced organizational values. *Ekonomska misao i praksa*, (2), 545–563.

2. Pearce, C. L., & Conger, J. A. (2003). All those years ago. In C. L. Pearce & J. A. Conger (Eds.), *Shared leadership: Reframing the hows and whys of leadership* (pp. 1–18). Thousand Oaks, CA: Sage.

3. Carton, A. M., Murphy, C., & Clark, J. R. (2014). A (blurry) vision of the future: How leader rhetoric about ultimate goals influences performance. *Academy of Management Journal, 57*(6), 1544–1570.

4. Birkinshaw, J., Foss, N. J., & Lindenberg, S. (2014). Combining purpose with profits. *MIT Sloan Management Review, 55*(3), 49.

5. Quinn, R. E., & Thakor, A. V. (2018, July–August). Creating a purpose-driven organization. *Harvard Business Review*, pp. 78–85.

6. See, for example, Carson, J. B., Tesluk, P. E., & Marrone, J. A. (2007). Shared leadership in teams: An investigation of antecedent conditions and performance. *Academy of Management Journal, 50*(5), 1217–1234.

7. Stogdill, R. M. (1948). Personal factors associated with leadership: A survey of the literature. *Journal of Psychology, 25*, 35–71.

8. Hersey, P., & Blanchard, K. H. (1969). Life-cycle theory of leadership. *Training and Development Journal, 23*, 26–34.

9. Dansereau, F., Graen, G. G., & Haga, W. (1975). A vertical dyad linkage approach to leadership in formal organizations. *Organizational Behavior and Human Performance, 13*, 46–78.

10. Rost, J. C. (1991). *Leadership for the 21st century.* New York: Praeger.

11. Bass, B. M., & Avolio, B. J. (1994). *Improving organizational effectiveness through transformational leadership.* Thousand Oaks, CA: Sage.

12. Amernic, J., Craig, R., & Tourish, D. (2007). The transformational leader as pedagogue, physician, architect, commander, and saint: Five root metaphors in Jack Welch's letters to stockholders of General Electric. *Human Relations, 60*(12), 1839–1872.

13. Greenleaf, R. K. (1970). *The servant as a leader.* Indianapolis: The Greenleaf Center.

14. Sendjaya, S., & Pekerti, A. (2010). Servant leadership as antecedent of trust in organizations. *Leadership & Organization Development Journal, 31*(7), 643–663.

15. Maccoby, M. (2000). Narcissistic leaders. *Harvard Business Review, 78*(1), 92–101.

16. Collins, J. (2001, January). Level 5 leadership: The triumph of humility and fierce resolve. *Harvard Business Review.*

17. For a summary of positive effects of proactive behavior in organizations, see Grant, A. M., Parker, S., & Collins, C. (2009). Getting credit for proactive behavior: Supervisor reactions depend on what you value and how you feel. *Personnel Psychology, 62*(1), 31–55.

18. Reiche, B. S., Cardona, P., Lee, Y. T., Canela, M. Á., Akinnukawe, E., Briscoe, J. P., … & Grenness, T. (2014). Why do managers engage in trustworthy

behavior? A multilevel cross-cultural study in 18 countries. *Personnel Psychology, 67*(1), 61–98.

19. Carson, J. B., Tesluk, P. E., & Marrone, J. A. (2007). Shared leadership in teams: An investigation of antecedent conditions and performance. *Academy of Management Journal, 50*(5), 1217–1234; Serban, A., & Roberts, A. J. (2016). Exploring antecedents and outcomes of shared leadership in a creative context: A mixed-methods approach. *The Leadership Quarterly, 27*(2), 181–199.

20. Carton, A. M., Murphy, C., & Clark, J. R. (2014). A (blurry) vision of the future: How leader rhetoric about ultimate goals influences performance. *Academy of Management Journal, 57*(6), 1544–1570.

21. Craig, N. (2018). *Leading from purpose.* New York, NY: Hachette Book Group.

22. George, B., McLean, A., & Craig, N. (2011). *Finding your true north: A personal guide* (Vol. 156). Hoboken, NJ: John Wiley & Sons.

23. Craig, N., & Snook, S. (2014). From purpose to impact. *Harvard Business Review, 92*(5), 104–111.

24. Michaelson, C., Pratt, M. G., Grant, A. M., & Dunn, C. P. (2014). Meaningful work: Connecting business ethics and organization studies. *Journal of Business Ethics, 121*(1), 77–90.

25. Craig, N., & Snook, S. (2014). From purpose to impact. *Harvard Business Review, 92*(5), 104–111.

26. Cardona, P. (2000). Transcendental leadership. *The Leadership & Organization Development Journal, 21*(4), 201–206.

27. Pérez López, J. A. (2014). *Foundations of management.* Madrid: Rialp.

28. Argandoña, A. (2003). Fostering values in organizations. *Journal of Business Ethics, 45*(1–2), 15–28.

29. Carson, J. B., Tesluk, P. E., & Marrone, J. A. (2007). Shared leadership in teams: An investigation of antecedent conditions and performance. *Academy of Management Journal, 50*(5), 1217–1234.

30. Reiche, B. S., Cardona, P., Lee, Y. T., Canela, M. Á., Akinnukawe, E., Briscoe, J. P., … & Grenness, T. (2014). Why do managers engage in trustworthy behavior? A multilevel cross-cultural study in 18 countries. *Personnel Psychology, 67*(1), 61–98.

31. Craig, N. (2018). *Leading from purpose.* New York, NY: Hachette Book Group.

32. Cardona, P., & Rey, C. (2008). *Management by missions.* New York: Palgrave Macmillan.

Part II

Creating Purpose-driven Organizations

6

Agile Purpose: Overcoming Bureaucracy

Carlos Rey, Nuno Pitta, Donatas Ramonas, and Phil Sotok

As the twenty-first century progresses, marked by a staggering increase in change, volatility, and complexity, many executives are having trouble resolving the tension between innovation and operational discipline. Some blame hierarchical structures for slowing down the decision-making process, generating excessive bureaucratization, and hindering innovation. This challenge is so difficult that it has led to several decades' worth of management experiments that completely challenge traditional organizations—democratic companies, podularity, liberated organizations, holacracy—but none of them are offering a clear answer.[1] In general terms, these supposed 'solutions' do not always fit within the natural development of an organization and its institutional configuration, and moreover, by themselves they are unable to solve the problems of bureaucracy.[2]

C. Rey (✉)
Universitat Internacional de Catalunya,
Barcelona, Spain
e-mail: carlosrey@uic.es

N. Pitta • P. Sotok
DPMC, Barcelona, Spain
e-mail: n.pitta@dpmc.es; psotok@dpmc.us

D. Ramonas
CRC Consulting, Vilnius, Lithuania
e-mail: donatas.ramonas@crc.lt

© The Author(s) 2019
C. Rey et al. (eds.), *Purpose-driven Organizations*,
https://doi.org/10.1007/978-3-030-17674-7_6

More recently, movements born from concepts such as 'agile organizations'[3] are exploring new ways to develop adaptable and responsive structures. But what is commonly underestimated in their practical development is that structures, per se, do not create the energy or sense of meaning that a dynamic marketplace requires. It is simply not enough to challenge traditional structures in order to gain agility in organizations. Indeed, the common denominator we find in successful cases of highly adaptive organizations is a high sense of purpose.

Think about some of the successful 'alternative organizations' that have been studied over recent years: Gore, Patagonia, Morning Star, and Zappos. As we see things, the key to their success does not come only from eliminating hierarchies, but from combining alternative structures with an overarching sense of purpose. All of these companies have served as good examples of purpose-driven organizations. Gore and Patagonia are commonly used as exemplars of humanistic management.[4] Morning Star, the tomato processing company in California that has 'no bosses', has been recognized by researchers as a highly purpose-driven organization,[5] as is Zappos, which claims that its purpose is 'to deliver happiness to the world'.[6] It is no coincidence then that researchers are finding a high sense of purpose as core to successful and highly adaptive organizations.[7] It is seen also at the foundation and creation of shared leadership.[8] This is why loss of purpose is frequently cited in cases of adaptive failure (e.g. Nokia[9]). Likewise, many attempts to create agile organizations fail because of a purposeless and disengaged workforce.

Hierarchy brings challenge (as with any human organization), but hierarchy is not the main problem. The underlying problem is that companies try to create more adaptative organizations by means of organizational forms that are themselves not structured around purpose. What companies need, rather, in order to gain agility in the new 'purpose economy',[10] is not the unnatural introduction of alien practices, but organic systems and structures that fit within their existing institutional configuration and purpose.[11] Purpose and agility have a fundamental interrelationship that requires a renewed understanding of traditional management practices.

Based on our research and consulting work, this chapter will offer an integrated view, one we refer to as 'agile purpose': the development of agile organizations by means of purpose-driven structures. First, we will show how purpose can be deployed into the management structure through the use of *missions* and further, of how to combine missions with forms of organizational agility in order to unleash the full potential of purpose.

Purpose and Missions

Activation of purpose through a compelling mission is considered by experts as fundamental for 'unleashing the power of purpose'.[12] This can be explained through the interplay of four basic management tools: missions, competences, objectives, and processes (see Table 6.1). The last three—processes, objectives, and competences—constitute the basic 'operating system' of a company. They represent the 'what and how' and relate to our tasks, achievements, and behaviors.

However, for purpose to prevail, it requires 'a new organizational form'[13] that moves beyond the traditional management tools of 'what and how'. It demands a form 'that does not presuppose homogeneity of background or tasks'. Purpose is like a new 'hardware' that demands a new 'software'. When management systems fail to support the development of purpose, then its development suffers because 'the systems ordinarily prevail'.[14] Many recent research findings are pointing in this direction.

Consider, for example, the research on goal framing. This theory argues that management systems based on objectives undermine the development of purpose, as they tend to focus on extrinsic gain and neglect the pro-social goals necessary for purpose development.[15] This is consistent with other recent research that shows the tendency of target setting to focus inward and discount external information,[16] promoting the 'dark side'[17] of goal setting that can motivate unethical behavior,[18] or increase the negative effect of goal-oriented management in turbulent environments.[19]

In a way, this limitation is intuitive. Just as we know one can complete a lot of tasks without meeting the given objective, one can meet various objectives without fulfilling any purpose. This is something we have seen, for example, in the damage certain financial companies and institutions caused by incentivizing their managers to achieve objectives that systematically sowed the seeds of the financial crises and subsequently damaged the entire world economy.

Many experts insist that the solution is not to eliminate objectives, but rather to develop a new 'cognitive/symbolic management' approach that fosters the operationalization of purpose in organizations.[20] As we see it, this new

Table 6.1 Basic management tools

Management tools	Related to
Missions	Impact
Competences	Behavior
Objectives	Achievements
Processes	Tasks

cognitive/symbolic management approach is grounded in the implementation of *missions*.

Corporate, Team, and Individual Missions

At the corporate level, purpose and missions are frequently used as interchangeable terms as both reside in the domain of 'why'. However, purpose and missions can also be quite different in substance. Purpose is generally described broadly, usually in one or two concepts. Missions are typically more concrete, reflecting the desired impact a company professes to its main stakeholders (customers, employees, shareholders, etc.).[21]

Missions are a form of *externalization of purpose* that make explicit the impact we have on others.[22] Missions help to turn purpose into a practical reality, solidifying purpose into specific commitments to specific beneficiaries. Missions, at the collective or individual level, answer the questions: What are the main beneficiaries of our/my job? What is the impact we/I want to have on them?

Think about the videos that many organizations offer, showing their impact on society. When companies are true to their purpose, these videos are a great source of energy and motivation. Missions are like these videos, telling every employee and team what they specifically do for others: a colleague, a friend, a customer, a supplier, or society. Missions are the sum impact that each employee makes for the other in their sphere of influence.

In our experience, the use of missions can be a very powerful and effective management tool, but only when its practice meets three fundamental conditions. First, missions must emanate from the intersection between personal and organizational purpose. They are not simply an intellectual construct, or a technical design. Missions come alive from purpose as they arise from the domain of the new logic of purpose. As a result, missions have little to no effect when developed in contexts dominated by the old logic of management. This is the fundamental reason why they have been ineffective in so many companies.[23] They are being used by companies that are not truly purpose driven. It is like having a software program that does not match the hardware. You can download it, but you cannot install it. If the company is not true to its purpose, missions are irrelevant. But if the company is true to its purpose, missions become of extreme importance.

The second condition is to ensure that the corporate missions are aligned with the *intra-organizational missions* (team and individual). As research has consistently demonstrated, the widespread practice of defining missions only at the corporate level is insufficient in helping employees understand how missions affect them personally, in their daily activities.[24] The corporate purpose needs to be deployed in the form of missions to every individual, providing a consistent framework for organizational alignment.[25] Expanding the presence of missions, as we see it, is a philosophy based on the principle of subsidiarity: matters should be handled at the most decentralized level. This principle, observed in the social and political arenas in many different cultures and countries, has been traditionally neglected in the theory of management and 'it has rarely been applied to business organization'.[26] However, it is the principle that resides in the new quest for purpose-driven organizations, as 'embedding subsidiarity in purpose would give employees the autonomy and support, when necessary, to make decisions that are purpose-driven'.[27] Intra-organizational missions make explicit to every individual and every team how their contribution impacts the company's mission[s], and ultimately its purpose (see Fig. 6.1).

The third condition is that missions must be evaluable. Many organizations take great effort to define their missions at a corporate, team, and individual levels, yet they fail to establish respective mechanisms to measure their attainment. When this happen, missions fall into the 'inspirational' category,

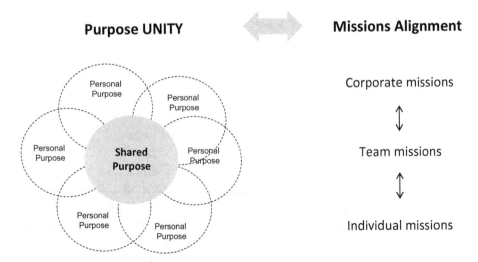

Fig. 6.1   Interplay between unity and alignment

becoming a public relations exercise or mere rhetoric. They lack having a tangible impact on its management. Implementing purpose by means of missions requires the discipline of measuring their performance to purpose. This is the case in Semillas Fitó, an international seed company based in Barcelona. They define their missions at the corporate and team levels and then use what they call 'mission scorecards' to monitor the progress of each mission relative to their corporate purpose.[28]

Aligned Autonomy

Missions constitute a fundamental tool to foster the equilibrium between alignment and autonomy. As missions emanate from purpose, they represent a 'higher level' of alignment than competences, objectives, or processes. By creating alignment through missions, organizations give structure to individual freedom, thereby increasing their capacity to see and respond to change. This alignment further helps both teams and individuals adapt and reconfigure their objectives and competences in a coordinated manner, without losing alignment to the company's purpose. Consider, for example, the case of Spotify. Along with the company's mission, each team has a long-term mission that is aligned with Spotify's overall mission as well as coordinated with other teams' missions. Through the alignment of missions, they create 'loosely coupled and tightly aligned' teams. As they say 'it is kind of like a jazz band. Although each musician is autonomous, they listen to each other and focus on the whole song together. That is how great music is created'. With missions, Spotify provides a combination of high levels of autonomy and alignment, while leaving freedom for processes, objectives, and competences to be reconfigured by individuals. They do this without losing the overall alignment to their purpose. This is called 'aligned autonomy'.[29]

Morning Star applies a similar approach. Their corporate mission is deployed in hundreds of personal missions—defined by its full-time and part-time employees. 'Missions are the cornerstone of Morning Star's management model' where 'you are responsible for the accomplishment of your mission and for acquiring the training, resources, and cooperation that you need to fulfill your mission'. By defining missions in this way, Morning Star has gained an overarching framework that makes possible 'shifting the focus from rule-driven compliance to peer-negotiated accountability'.[30]

The capacity of missions to align organizations at a 'higher level' can also be seen in the highly complex organizations found in healthcare, where processes are systematized and interdependent. Missions at different levels and functions (e.g. physicians, nurses, and managers) can support each group's 'understanding of the others' mission, helping the integration of work and enhancing a shared sense of purpose.[31] In this way, the coordination of missions overcomes the limitations of bureaucracy, giving more freedom to act within hierarchical structures. Take the case of Biok, for example, a leading cosmetics company in the Baltic region. They define missions at various levels of the company which helps them to move forward with new products into new markets with much more speed, while staying true to the spirit of the purpose along the way.[32] Another case is that of the multinational oil company Repsol. They evaluate their alignment to missions—deployed by each department—by examining any conflicting issues (e.g. between sales and operations) and turning those into joint objectives. This practice facilitates cooperation, and even sacrifice when required. By promoting alignment at a 'higher level' of purpose, the coordination of missions helped Repsol to break silos and avoid escalating conflicts, changing drastically the levels of communication among departments, middle management, and employees.[33]

Missions alignment can also guide the deployment of objectives, incorporating more agile and adaptive practices. We are used to understanding the alignment of objectives as a top-down process. But in reality, there are other ways to align objectives that can be more productive and flexible. These are, for example, peer negotiation (where objectives get discussed by teams) or bottom-up (where lower-level employees become the primary source of setting objectives). With missions, whether arrived at from top-down, bottom-up, or peer-to-peer, these practices are not exclusive but mutually reinforcing. Consider the case of the sales force of Alpha Omega, in Israel. In the overall context of missions alignment, base-line employees propose their objectives, then discuss in small groups with peers, and finally, agree with managers who aggregate and coordinate the objectives.[34] This is the case as well for NalonChem, where a similar missions alignment process 'helped to reduce the time of setting objectives by half'.[35]

Finally, missions alignment helps to connect the organization to its stakeholders by setting objectives in what is called an 'outside in' approach.[36] This approach considers actual market trends and needs, rather than taking a company's prior year performance as the starting point. Thus, by combining missions with data from the marketplace, goals become more ambitious and adjustable, providing guidance, autonomy, and orientation for teams and individuals to define better objectives.[37]

Agile Structures and Purpose

From a practical point of view, organizations can realize the benefits that emerge when their people are both autonomous and aligned in what we call the 'agile purpose chart'. It shows the various outcomes that occur when we integrate missions into operational *reliability* and *adaptability*.[38] Reliability refers to undertakings such as obtaining expected results, adjusting standards, meeting budgets, managing risk, following strategy, and so on, while adaptability refers to the autonomy of our work, the capacity for innovation, the ability to adapt to customer needs, or the improvement of processes, to name a few. When team and individual missions are combined with reliability and adaptability, we set the stage for a different kind of organizational structure. One that <u>simultaneously</u> develops and integrates into a holistic model. This model includes the concurrent combination of four hierarchical and self-managed organizational forms: governance hierarchy, management hierarchy, self-managed teams and self-managed networks (see Fig. 6.2).

Today, most companies continue to define themselves primarily by hierarchical designs. However, in reality, usually all four are present in purpose-driven companies. These four designs are indeed natural developments of purpose-driven organizations. The military is a good example of this. Despite their hierarchical structures, their collective high sense of purpose forms itself into a

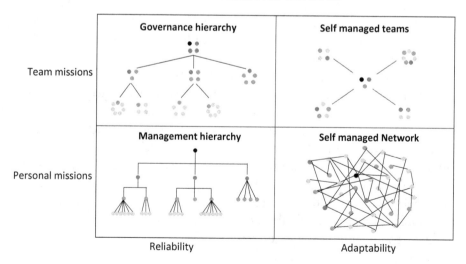

Fig. 6.2 Illustration of an agile purpose chart

well-orchestrated network of self-managed teams.[39] Or in the case of Wikipedia: although it is a self-managed network of individuals, it requires some form of hierarchy for 'legitimate authority' to govern the purpose of the organization.[40] In our experience, the model we present here helps to outline the actual potential residing in purpose-driven organizations. In short, it provides a framework in which each company can find its natural place, combining the hierarchical and non-hierarchical forms to best suit its purpose and institutional requirements. Every company needs to find its particular equilibrium in the use of the four designs mentioned above, and avoid the least productive scenarios residing on the fringes.

Through the framework, we have seen companies dramatically increase their ability to adapt to change, making profound transformations while, at the same time, reinforcing their commitment to the outlined purpose. For Jimenez Maña, the automobile spare parts company in Andalusia, this was indeed the case. The company initiated a significant transformation to its business by re-focusing efforts and activities around its true comparative advantage. It did so without the elimination of hierarchies. Instead, they combined hierarchical and self-managed structures, and facilitated their coordination and consistency through the use missions, which served as their source of overall alignment. To this end, the company employed self-managed teams and networks as a primary way of organizing their operations. Questions such as the definition of the strategy, the coordination of missions, or the establishment of compensation are addressed through the governance and management hierarchy.[41]

In our experience, the agile purpose chart increases an organization's ability to sense and react to change without losing its alignment to purpose. Such a model provides a legitimate source of authority to individuals and teams, empowering them not by the chain of command but primarily by purpose. It offers enormous potential for the development of organizations, helping to solidify purpose while enhancing motivation, adaptability, and agility. It is an answer to the question that organizational theorists struggle with when confronting a world of relentless change, ferocious competition, and unstoppable innovation: 'How do we build organizations that deserve the extraordinary gifts that our employees bring to work?'[42] The agile purpose chart helps people find their 'right place' in organizations by allowing them to express their personal purpose at work. This means giving individuals what is called 'freedom within a framework', allowing them the space to breathe, grow, and evolve within the company's changing needs.[43]

The agile purpose chart, in the broadest sense, provides a much deeper view of the organization as well as the person. Here each employee feels and acts as the true protagonist of their work, and managers know how to handle, with skill, the delicate balance that exists between their role as leaders and their duty as bosses. Missions ultimately help incorporate the new logic of purpose that views employees from a transcendent perspective, capable of acting for reasons other than the mere satisfaction of their own needs. This now becomes the new point of departure, that is, when we see the organization through the lens of purpose we ultimately see the person through this same lens. Their reason for being shines because they are part of a high-purpose environment where they can more easily respond to their calling and give of themselves, freely and meaningfully in concert with others, toward a common end.

Notes

1. Gulati, R. (2018). Structure that's not stifling. *Harvard Business Review, 96*(3), 68–79.
2. Hamel, G., & Zanini, M. (2016). Top-down solutions like holacracy won't fix bureaucracy. *Harvard Business Review.*
3. Rigby, D. K., Sutherland, J., & Noble, A. (2018). Agile at scale. *Harvard Business Review.*
4. https://vimeo.com/114733511. Retrieved September 27, 2018.
5. Hamel, G. (2011). First, let's fire all the managers. *Harvard Business Review, 89*(12), 48–60.
6. Forbes 2013/11/04/. Retrieved from https://www.forbes.com/sites/skollworldforum/2013/11/04/gamechangers-the-worlds-top-purpose-driven-organizations/#73ed2dc377b6
7. Fjeldstad, Ø. D., Snow, C. C., Miles, R. E., & Lettl, C. (2012). The architecture of collaboration. *Strategic Management Journal, 33*(6), 734–750.
8. Carson, J. B., Tesluk, P. E., & Marrone, J. A. (2007). Shared leadership in teams: An investigation of antecedent conditions and performance. *Academy of Management Journal, 50*(5), 1217–1234.
9. Chevreux, L., Lopez, J., & Mesnard, X. (2017). The best companies know how to balance strategy and purpose. *Harvard Business Review.*
10. Hurst, A. (2016). *The purpose economy: How your desire for impact, personal growth and community is changing the world.* Elevate Publishing.
11. Mackey, J., & Sisodia, R. (2014). *Conscious capitalism: Liberating the heroic spirit of business.* Harvard Business Review Press.
12. Ibidem.
13. Adler, P. S., & Heckscher, C. (2018). Collaboration as an organization design for shared purpose. In *Toward permeable boundaries of organizations?* (pp. 81–111). London: Emerald Publishing Limited.
14. Laloux, F. (2014). *Reinventing organizations: A guide to creating organizations inspired by the next stage in human consciousness.* Brussels: Nelson Parker.

15. Birkinshaw, J., Foss, N. J., & Lindenberg, S. (2014). Combining purpose with profits. *MIT Sloan Management Review, 55*(3), 49.
16. Aranda, C., Arellano, J., & Davila, A. (2017). Organizational learning in target setting. *Academy of Management Journal, 60*(3), 1189–1211.
17. Niven, K., & Healy, C. (2016). Susceptibility to the 'dark side' of goal-setting: Does moral justification influence the effect of goals on unethical behaviour? *Journal of Business Ethics, 137*(1), 115–127.
18. Schweitzer, M. E., Ordóñez, L., & Douma, B. (2004). Goal setting as a motivator of unethical behavior. *Academy of Management Journal, 47*(3), 422–432.
19. Harms, R., Reschke, C. H., Kraus, S., & Fink, M. (2010). Antecedents of innovation and growth: Analysing the impact of entrepreneurial orientation and goal-oriented management. *International Journal of Technology Management, 52*(1/2), 135–152.
20. Lindenberg, S., & Foss, N. J. (2011). Managing joint production motivation: The role of goal framing and governance mechanisms. *Academy of Management Review, 36*(3), 500–525.
21. Bartkus, B. R., & Glassman, M. (2008). Do firms practice what they preach? The relationship between mission statements and stakeholder management. *Journal of Business Ethics, 83*(2), 207–216.
22. Bart, C. K., Bontis, N., & Taggar, S. (2001). A model of the impact of mission statements on firm performance. *Management Decision, 39*(1), 19–35.
23. Bartkus, B. R., & Glassman, M. (2008). Do firms practice what they preach? The relationship between mission statements and stakeholder management. *Journal of Business Ethics, 83*(2), 207–216.
24. Kopaneva, I., & Sias, P. M. (2015). Lost in translation: Employee and organizational constructions of mission and vision. *Management Communication Quarterly, 29*(3), 358–384.
25. Cardona, P., & Rey, C. (2008). *Management by missions*. New York: Palgrave Macmillan.
26. Melé, D. (2005). Exploring the principle of subsidiarity in organisational forms. *Journal of Business Ethics, 60*(3), 293–305.
27. Hollensbe, E., Wookey, C., Hickey, L., George, G., & Nichols, C. V. (2014). Organizations with purpose. *Academy of Management Journal, 57*(5), 1227–1234.
28. https://www.youtube.com/watch?v=aGaFeld7dGc. Retrieved January 30, 2019.
29. Ibidem.
30. https://labs.spotify.com/2014/03/27/spotify-engineering-culture-part-1/. Retrieved September 4, 2018.
31. Pires, J. F., Rey, C., Mas-Machuca, M., & Bastons, M. (2016). Management by missions in the healthcare sector. *Revista de Calidad Asistencial, 31*(4), 239–242.

32. https://www.youtube.com/watch?v=xI1Cg2FkrxM. Retrieved January 30, 2019.

33. Cardona, P., Rey, C., & Carmona, P. H. (2012). Caso Repsol Portuguesa: cómo vencer la resistencia al cambio. *Harvard Deusto Business Review*, (212), 38–47.

34. Cardona, P., & Rey, C. (2008). *Management by missions*. New York: Palgrave Macmillan.

35. https://www.youtube.com/user/catedraDpm/search?query=nalon. Retrieved November 3, 2018.

36. Hamel, G., & Zanini, M. (2018). The end of bureaucracy. *Harvard Business Review*.

37. Rey, C., Chinchilla, N., & Pitta, N. (2017). Objectives are SMART, missions are WISE: Employees with purpose, *IESE Insight*, No. 33, Second Quarter 2017, pp. 45–51.

38. Bernstein, E., Bunch, J., Canner, N., & Lee, M. (2016). Beyond the holacracy hype. *Harvard Business Review, 94*(7), 8.

39. Fussell, C., & Goodyear, C. W. (2017). *One mission: How leaders build a team of teams*. Penguin.

40. For the question on when and how managers must use legitimate power over self-managed work see: Klapper, H., & Reitzig, M. (2018). On the effects of authority on peer motivation: Learning from Wikipedia. *Strategic Management Journal*.

41. https://www.youtube.com/watch?v=BWh4BCKvQaA. Retrieved January 30, 2019.

42. Hamel, G. (2012). *What matters now: How to win in a world of relentless change, ferocious competition, and unstoppable innovation*. John Wiley & Sons.

43. Gulati, R. (2018). Structure that's not stifling. *Harvard Business Review, 96*(3), 68–79.

7

Key Factors in Purpose Internalization

Carlos Rey, Frederic Marimon, and Marta Mas-Machuca

As discussed in previous chapters, excelling at purpose internalization is a common trait of purpose-driven companies. *Purpose internalization* occurs when an organization's members integrate their personal beliefs and motivations with the organization's purpose. We also know from research done by The Harvard Business School[1] that clarity of purpose throughout the organization has a positive impact on performance, suggesting that once purpose is discovered it must be clearly placed at the center of the company's narrative.

For such a feat to occur, companies typically embark on activities that foster an employee's purpose internalization through several means, such as videos, testimonies, and speeches. However, while defining and communicating your organization's purpose is one thing, getting your teams to internalize its meaning and scope is quite another. As we have seen in many cases, efforts to communicate the purpose do not always lead to employees taking true "ownership" of it. This was the case of a multinational IT solutions provider in Europe. The company had a great reputation in the marketplace, ranking

C. Rey (✉)
Universitat Internacional de Catalunya,
Barcelona, Spain
e-mail: carlosrey@uic.es

F. Marimon • M. Mas-Machuca
Department of Economy and Business Organization, Universitat Internacional de Catalunya, Barcelona, Spain
e-mail: fmarimon@uic.es; mmas@uic.es

© The Author(s) 2019
C. Rey et al. (eds.), *Purpose-driven Organizations*,
https://doi.org/10.1007/978-3-030-17674-7_7

high on the "best places to work" survey. However, it received poor results when graded on the degree to which its purpose was internalized among its employees. As a result, the company embarked on an intensive campaign to communicate its purpose. They used screensavers, videos, and posters throughout the office. The management gave inspiring speeches, referring often to the purpose and published articles about it in the company's internal magazine. Yet, after two years, the degree to which its purpose had been internalized was measured again and the same poor results were obtained.

Creating environments that enhance purpose internalization is indeed an art. However, a certain dose of science can help this art become much more effective. Start by asking, which means of communication might be most effective in transmitting the purpose and of those, which ones might best help your employees buy into the purpose?

To answer this questions, we developed a model for assessing purpose internalization across seven dimensions (see Table 7.1). Based on our empirical research, recently published in Industrial Management and Data Systems,[2] we identified the best criteria for effective purpose communication. The results,

Table 7.1 Significance of the seven dimensions of purpose internalization

1. Knowledge of the purpose	Significant
The extent to which the employees know the purpose and are capable of explaining it in their own words.	
2. Understanding the importance of the purpose	Significant
The extent to which the employees feel the purpose is relevant to them and for society.	
3. Visible commitment from leadership (overlaps with 5)	Significant
The extent to which the managers of a company are committed to the purpose and make their decisions accordingly, thus providing visibility through their actions of their engagement to the purpose.	(most relevant)
4. Visible commitment of co-workers	Significant
The extent to which employees feel that their colleagues are committed to the purpose.	(most relevant)
5. Perceived coherence between purpose and practice (overlaps with 3)	Significant (most relevant)
The extent to which employees perceive that company decisions and day-to-day actions are consistent with the purpose.	
6. Reflecting on the purpose	Significant
The extent to which employees participate in conceptualizing and giving their opinions relative to the purpose.	
7. Frequently recalling the purpose	Non-significant
The extent to which a company formally and regularly communicates their purpose (placards, videos, speeches, etc.)	

We consider "most relevant" load values > 0,7

explained in this chapter along with practical examples and implications, identified six effective dimensions and one that, surprisingly, despite its common use, is ineffective.

Knowledge of the Purpose

Simple as it sounds, people must have explicit knowledge and a clear understanding of the purpose to the extent that they are able to explain it in their own words. Several studies demonstrate the need for purpose to be clearly communicated,[3] paying special attention to how the message is interpreted, as well as to the feelings and emotions that the message provokes. Take for example, the pharmaceutical company Ferrer, whose purpose "to advance the well-being in society" has been made accessible and meaningful to all employees according to its HR manager, "thanks to the intensive communication of this simple statement." It has helped everyone, "from managers to factory employees, we use a common language when talking about our purpose." Another example is that of ISS, the Danish Facility Services company. They communicate their purpose to a workforce of half a million people in a very straight forward way: "we facilitate our customer's purpose." To better bring this purpose to its employees, ISS engages in emotional storytelling and talking about internal examples of how this has been accomplished. This helps all workers, from the cleaning staff to the maintenance team to the catering crew, who clearly understand their roles in living out this purpose through the work they do.[4]

When clear communication of the purpose and its content is lacking, organizations are more likely to develop confused messages,[5] leading to ambiguity and lack of awareness. In such organizations employees struggle to explain their company's purpose in their own words.

Understanding the Importance of the Purpose

One way of accomplishing this is to make the purpose relatable to a greater cause and consistent with a generally accepted value system. It must be accepted as the correct way to think and act. For this reason, it is necessary to clearly explain that the company's purpose is good for not only employees but society at large.[6] In order that employees understand the importance and need of purpose, organizations should consider using comprehensive arguments that relate the purpose to socially accepted values. A good example of this is the training program for managers at Bimbo.[7] Before explaining the company's purpose, employees are encouraged to reflect upon their own purpose in life and the benefits of having one. Similarly, at Vygon, a French medical device company, the company periodically publishes stories on their intranet about people who achieved great feats and benefits thanks to a clear purpose.[8]

This dimension should not be ignored, because if employees fail to understand the importance and need for a purpose, it will play no role in their personal beliefs and values. In this case, purpose runs the risk of being perceived as "just another fad" or worse, seen by employees as a marketing ploy, out of context with the organization's various communication strategies.

Visible Commitment from Leadership

As suggested by many, "communicating purpose is the most central of all leadership behaviors"[9] with the ability of employees to commit to purpose depending on this dimension. We have all seen examples of organizations that profess one thing but act completely different. It destroys credibility. This is equally true for purpose. The relevance of purpose is not so much the appeal of the message but the testimony as to its significance by company leaders.[10] All too often, employees tend to appreciate their company's purpose but need confirmation that their "bosses" are truly committed in order to accept it. When a leader communicates the purpose with authenticity and constancy employees begin to believe in the purpose themselves: "the purpose is signaled from the top, and unfolds from the bottom."[11]

Our research showed that commitment, at the managerial level, had the greatest impact on whether or not purpose was internalized and positively embraced. These results are extremely important for their practical implications. Purpose has become such a popular topic that, "even leaders who don't fully believe face pressure from board members, investors, employees, and other stakeholders to communicate a higher purpose."[12] But this would be completely ineffective as purpose requires deep engagement of managers. This might seem to be a simple idea, but it is not. Many companies devote significant resources and time to achieve a technically impressive campaign because they believe this singular approach is what leads to success. Yet, if employees still do not see a real commitment by the leadership to the message, then the communication will be ineffective. Even more troubling is that this approach could be fatally discouraging for employees who want to believe the message, because it will negatively impact trust in future communications coming from the top. The lack of trust in an organization's message can turn into a general lack of trust in its managers, and erode even further the morale of the employees, affecting their motivation and commitment. In short, the most powerful communication medium is the authentic behavior of the company's managers and leaders. This matters most.

For the founder of Bimbo, this has always been clear.[13] He holds that anyone in management positions should be a "leader of the purpose" and thus show his or her own responsibility and commitment to it. Something similar can be seen at the tier one automotive component supplier, HUF Portuguesa.[14] Here, the purpose is at the center of the performance evaluation model by which all employees are graded. In every company in which we have worked, commitment from the managers is necessary for creating interdependent contributions. Without commitment, the purpose lacks legitimacy and will not be shared by employees.

Visible Commitment of Co-workers

Seeing the commitment of those around us to the company's purpose is significant because it forms the foundation of corporate identity and its shared belief system. For employees to internalize purpose, they must be convinced of the commitment of others in the organization, especially those with whom they interact regularly.[15] This means we must be conscious of how purpose is ingrained in the company's culture.[16]

This dimension is considered by many to be a highly effective means for purpose to reach each and every employee more deeply. At JJC, a construction company in Peru, communicating their purpose is usually accompanied by images, examples, or phrases where employees show their personal commitment to the corporate purpose. This is similar at Jimenez Maña, a medium size company of automobile spare parts in Andalucía (Spain), where periodic videos and testimonies of employees appear on their intranet explaining the company's purpose and how it contributes to their work.

Our results show that a true test of management's commitment is the "perceived commitment of their co-workers." These findings are consistent with the idea that shared purpose requires shared leadership, and this serves to "demystify the notion of charismatic/transformational leadership."[17] If employees do not see this commitment in their co-workers, it can lead to a sense that the company's purpose is something abstract, and that it does not necessarily affect them personally.

Perceived Coherence Between Purpose and Practice

Coherence is present to the extent that an organization's daily actions and practices, experienced by employees, are aligned with the principles and direction set forth by its purpose. When companies are true to purpose, the daily activities of the organization will naturally provide ample evidence of the company's alignment to purpose. This is true for ISS, the Facility services provider, where the most seemingly trivial events, such as receiving a "thank-you" from a client, is communicated throughout the entire company as a sign of coherence to purpose. This is especially relevant when making difficult decisions that put the purpose to test, as may arise when a company faces the need for layoffs or fallout related to a public relations incident. The way the company acts in these situations, and equally important, how this is perceived by its employees, is crucial to the development of purpose.[18]

When a company truly lives its purpose, it becomes a "force" that elevates employee engagement. But if employees do not perceive coherence between purpose and practice, the purpose will lose credibility. Such a loss may occur due to ignorance or poor communication, especially among those employees who have limited knowledge about the general operations of the company. Hence it is important that the company "make a connection" by showing employees how their efforts benefit others.[19]

Our empirical analysis shows that perceived coherence between purpose and practice is significant to effective purpose internalization. However, we must note that, from the employees' perspective, point number 3 listed as *visible commitment from leadership* is identical to point number 5 *perceived coherence between purpose and practice* (see Table 7.1). In other words, employees identify the company's coherence with the management's commitment. Accordingly, both dimensions can be combined and considered jointly. This is consistent with the interconnection between internalization and implementation discussed in previous chapters.[20] Even companies that practice their purpose, such as a healthcare company that aims to "improve people's lives," must ensure its employees see a commitment by top management to this purpose and if this is not the case (e.g., if they think that the managers only care about money), the company will be perceived as incoherent (or hypocritical) by its employees.

Reflecting on the Purpose

For the purpose to come to life within an organization, there needs to be a means for people to reflect upon it. That is to say, it is not enough for only the top executives to consider the purpose, but rather it must be carried out consistently by all members of the company in such a way that it fosters a two-way communication. This is evident at the beauty products company, Biok, in Lithuania, where the various departments and areas engage each month in discussions about their purpose as well as their progress relative to its fulfillment.[21] This is similar to a practice done at Alpha Omega, a high-tech neuroscience company in Israel, where employees all over the world are brought together in small groups to reflect upon their specific contribution to the purpose of the company.[22] This level of intentional communication around purpose creates a positive environment, where employees are able to express their opinions about the purpose while at the same time build trust. Without such reflection, the purpose becomes what we might call an "apparent purpose" (or non-reflective), limiting it to a mere symbolic incorporation[23] where employees regard the company's purpose as a formality, but do not internalize its meaning.

Frequently Recalling the Purpose

In our original research, we considered this dimension based on the belief that frequently recalling the purpose ensures it will be ever present in the company's and employee's internal dialogues. This is typically relayed through means such as posters, screensavers, short company-wide email messages, and so on. With these actions, the company seizes the opportunity, every day, to remind its people of its purpose. In this initial research, we considered that the image evoked by the purpose would be a source of employee satisfaction because when a purpose is authentic and linked to personal values and beliefs, people welcome reminders of that which "gives meaning" to their actions and efforts.

However, our analysis indicates that this is not significant for purpose internalization. We invite the reader to carefully consider these findings. Certainly, a practice such as this can be useful in the early stages of a new purpose communication or when there are significant changes in the purpose, but only as a reinforcement of the dimension stated as point number 1, *knowing the content of purpose*. Because a communication plan that is solely based on recalling the purpose will be completely ineffective for its internalization. Indeed, companies that excel in the other six dimensions will have no need to embark on such specific recollection practices, since the internal dialogue will naturally lead to keeping the purpose alive.

Overall Effective Internalization

The implications of this research are clear: organizations must move beyond mere tactics with regard to purpose communication, and guarantee that employees experience its essence in the workplace. In other words, a company's communication must be oriented to create the necessary environment in which the purpose can flourish and ultimately become shared by all its employees. In this sense, the six significant dimensions identified in our research offer a guide for getting the environment right. Indeed, although they have been presented here independently, in practice they are rarely isolated. For instance, when a CEO explains the company's purpose to her employees, she simultaneously reinforces both the "knowledge of" and "commitment to" the purpose. In fact, one clear recommendation from our research is that the dimensions must be developed coincidingly instead of employing only a few in piecemeal fashion. That is, if the company focuses on one or two dimensions alone, effective purpose communication is not likely to be achieved.

As a rule of thumb, our advice is to use the greatest possible number of dimensions discussed in this chapter. Every significant event of the company can be an opportunity to deploy some or even all of the dimensions, reinforcing their joint effectiveness and enhancing consistency in purpose internalization.

Notes

1. Gartenberg, C., Prat, A., & Serafeim, G. (2019). Corporate purpose and financial performance. *Organization Science*.
2. Marimon, F., Mas-Machuca, M., & Rey, C. (2016). Assessing the internalization of the mission. *Industrial Management & Data Systems, 116*(1), 170–187.
3. Kopaneva, I., & Sias, P. M. (2015). Lost in translation: Employee and organizational constructions of mission and vision. *Management Communication Quarterly, 29*(3), 358–384.
4. https://www.youtube.com/watch?v=z9oMHg6cYqs. Retrieved January 30, 2019.

5. Kaplan, S. (2008). Framing contests: Strategy making under uncertainty. *Organization Science, 19*(5), 729–752.

6. Carton, A. M. (2018). "I'm not mopping the floors, I'm putting a man on the moon": How NASA leaders enhanced the meaningfulness of work by changing the meaning of work. *Administrative Science Quarterly, 63*(2), 323–369.

7. Worldwide leading bakery Mexican multinational with more than 130,000 employees.

8. https://www.youtube.com/watch?v=aPMnQHzqZGM&list=PLUOl1IsE77 bwsfbV9IRbt4GYaFNRlaCCM&index=3. Retrieved January 30, 2019.

9. Carton, A. M., Murphy, C., & Clark, J. R. (2014). A (blurry) vision of the future: How leader rhetoric about ultimate goals influences performance. *Academy of Management Journal, 57*(6), 1544–1570.

10. Hollensbe, E., Wookey, C., Hickey, L., George, G., & Nichols, C. V. (2014). Organizations with purpose. *Academy of Management Journal, 57*(5), 1227–1234.

11. Quinn, R. E., & Thakor, A. V. (2018, July–August). Creating a Purpose-Driven Organization. *Harvard Business Review*, pp. 78–85.

12. Ibidem.

13. Lorenzo Servitje (1918–2017).

14. https://www.youtube.com/watch?v=QftQxPKhqG8. Retrieved January 30, 2019.

15. White, A., Yakis-Douglas, B., Helanummi-Cole, H., & Ventresca, M. (2017). Purpose-led organization: "Saint Antony" reflects on the idea of organizational purpose, in principle and practice. *Journal of Management Inquiry, 26*(1), 101–107.

16. Almandoz, J., Lee, Y., & Ribera, A. (2018). Unleashing the power of purpose: 5 steps to transform your business, *IESE Insight*, 37, Second Quarter, 44–51.

17. Bono, J. E., & Judge, T. A. (2003). Self-concordance at work: Toward understanding the motivational effects of transformational leaders. *Academy of Management Journal, 46*(5), 554–571.

18. Birkinshaw, J., Foss, N. J., & Lindenberg, S. (2014). Combining purpose with profits. *MIT Sloan Management Review, 55*(3), 49.

19. Grant, A. M. (2012). Leading with meaning: Beneficiary contact, prosocial impact, and the performance effects of transformational leadership. *Academy of Management Journal, 55*(2), 458–476.

20. See Chap. 3.

21. https://www.youtube.com/watch?v=xI1Cg2FkrxM. Retrieved January 30, 2019.

22. https://www.youtube.com/watch?v=ejLoKiBzL94&t=237s. Retrieved January 30, 2019.

23. Gondo, M. B., & Amis, J. M. (2013). Variations in practice adoption: The roles of conscious reflection and discourse. *Academy of Management Review, 38*(2), 229–247.

8

Nurturing Personal Purpose at Work

Carlos Rey, Juan Almandoz, and Alex Montaner

Every human being seeks a purpose, a "why." Psychologists describe it as one of the main factors of resilience to survive under extreme circumstances. Viktor Frankl, an Austrian psychiatrist of Jewish origin, discovered in Auschwitz that having a purpose in life, something important to live for, contributed enormously to staying alive in the Nazi concentration camps. Researchers of positive psychology, among others, attribute having a purpose in life as one of the first causes of happiness, understood as "eudaimonia."

In a world that is in constant flux, where the path to follow is unclear, and where it can be hard to tell right from wrong, having a guiding purpose can be life changing. When people discover their purpose and live accordingly, their existence becomes more authentic and meaningful. Consciously or unconsciously, people seek to understand their purpose in order to reach and drive toward their full potential.

C. Rey (✉)
Universitat Internacional de Catalunya,
Barcelona, Spain
e-mail: carlosrey@uic.es

J. Almandoz
Department of Managing People in Organizations, IESE Business School,
Barcelona, Spain
e-mail: JAlmandoz@iese.edu

A. Montaner
DPMC, Barcelona, Spain
e-mail: a.montaner@dpmc.es

© The Author(s) 2019
C. Rey et al. (eds.), *Purpose-driven Organizations*,
https://doi.org/10.1007/978-3-030-17674-7_8

In today's corporate world, the idea of a personal purpose at work—a "why" to guide our efforts and dreams—is increasingly making its way into companies. By clarifying a purpose, people find greater meaning in their work, thus improving their motivation, efficiency, and ability to lead. Nowadays, an increasing number of companies are well aware of this and, through training programs and coaching, they invite their managers to be thoughtful about their purpose. They believe that, to be authentic leaders, managers must be able to, first and foremost, identify their own purpose. In some of these programs, some people write their purpose down and keep it in their wallet; others draw it or represent it with concepts and ideas. In other programs, people are asked to write a song about their purpose!

Reflecting on the purpose of one's work is a highly rewarding and inspiring exercise that can not only help one make better use of his or her abilities, but also serve as a guide in discerning future decisions. This exercise also helps to harmonize the purpose of the individual with that of the organization, which results in greater job satisfaction and quality of work. However, experience also shows that one's purpose tends to weaken over time, running the risk of being forgotten altogether when not properly nurtured.

The root of this problem is often a weak perspective of what purpose really entails, and what activities help to drive its development. Of course, the path to purpose does not end with a slogan, drawing, or plaque. Rather, defining one's purpose is merely where the path begins. What should one do to keep purpose *alive* over time?

Based on our experience and research, this chapter attempts to present a holistic model for personal purpose, and the processes that drive its development. With our model, we hope to provide a design framework for the development of programs and initiatives that center around purpose at work. However, it is only a model, and as such it is necessarily incomplete. Many nuances are missing or are not treated here with the depth they deserve. But we are satisfied that our recommendations cover the main dimensions of purpose at work and will act to stimulate its future development.

Head, Heart, and Hands

Many experts explain purpose as our raison d'être (our reason for being) or in other words, our "why," being the essence of what we bring to this world. But purpose is not born from just any "why"—one that might only subjectively explain a person's actions. Rather, purpose reflects the identity of a person objectively, in terms of what they actually do. In some cases, for example, this identity can be linked to practicing a recognized profession, one that contributes to the well-being of society. Objectively, that purpose would transcend the motivation of the person practicing such a profession. Take a doctor, for instance, who might have several motivations for her work, whether that be to make money, to be the best doctor in the hospital and gain recognition, or simply, to pursue a career. While the perception of herself as a doctor can be characterized by other elements such as her degree, her knowledge, the clinical methods she uses, as a doctor, none of these are her purpose. When we talk about purpose, a person's degree, knowledge, or even their accolades are rather irrelevant. What matters is that which most *characterizes her as a doctor*: to heal people, to save lives.

Although all doctors share an objective purpose because they belong to the same profession, it is also true that each person is unique and immersed in a different context. Therefore, subjectively the "why" can also be something intimate and unique for each person, linked to one's own subjective identity and, at the same time, open to others, and to the satisfaction of the needs of others.

Much like we have seen from organizational purpose, from the subjective perspective of the individual, the purpose is not a monolithic idea. Rather, an individual will have a purpose that entails three interdependent dimensions. The first dimension reflects the knowledge that each person has of their own purpose; the second is the practical implementation of the action, and the third is the motivation that drives people to carry out that purpose. These three dimensions can be symbolized in three fundamental parts of the human body: head, heart, and hands (see Fig. 8.1).

Head: In order to live our purpose, we need not only to know it but also to know how to communicate it. In other words, when we understand our purpose and are able to express its contents and meaning, in our own unique way, then it comes to life and starts to answer the age-old questions of: Why and for whom am I here? Who do I serve, or should I serve, and how? These are deeply personal questions and ones that we alone should freely answer for ourselves. It is not critical that our purpose be written down, but simply that we know it and that we are able to explain it (even if we explain it only to ourselves).

Hands: However, purpose is not knowledge alone, like an algebra problem that ends once solved. Nor is it like an inspiring slogan that is hung from the office walls for further contemplation. Rather, a proper understanding of purpose is to recognize that it also leads us to action. In fact, many say that, in order to truly know someone's purpose, look to their actions. Purposeful

Fig. 8.1 Holistic conceptualization of purpose (Source: Adapted from Rey, C., & Bastons, M. (2018). Three dimensions of effective mission implementation. *Long Range Planning, 51*(4), 580–585. / Graphic Design: Reproduced with permission from Freeland Communication Studio SL)

action is in itself an essential part of purpose. Without it, our purpose is incomplete. If our purpose is not carried out through our deeds, then indeed we have no purpose at all.

Heart: And finally, for purpose to be empowering, it must transcend both our knowledge and action. Purpose is energy, will, impulse; it is the inner force or motivation that orders and drives our internal potential—our values, beliefs, desires, affections, and feelings. When we compare our purpose to another person's we find that ours resonates internally and compels us to act. Another person's purpose does not have this same effect on us, although it might be somewhat inspiring. In fact, when we discover the energy in another person's purpose, it is likely that there is a connection to certain aspects of our own. This dimension of purpose moves us. We come to see our purpose as not only a responsibility to fulfill, but as something that is born from within, deeply personal and motivating.

Coherence, Authenticity, and Integrity

Our purpose is internalized and sustained when these three dimensions— heart, head, and hands—are linked, respectively, through coherence, authenticity, and integrity (Fig. 8.2). We define these words in the following way.

Coherence is defined as the fit between knowledge and action—between what we define as our purpose and what we actually do. When we are coherent with our purpose, it shows through meaningful practical deeds. Coherence entails the deployment of purpose in ambitious and realistic commitments

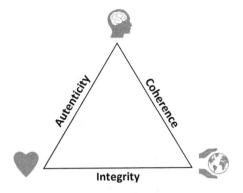

Fig. 8.2 Fit between the three dimensions of purpose (Graphic Design: Reproduced with permission from Freeland Communication Studio SL)

that are adaptable to our personal capabilities as well as our surrounding circumstances.

Authenticity is the fit between knowledge and motivation. It is the connection between what we define as our purpose and what really moves us internally. It considers the values, beliefs, and feelings that feed into our purpose. No doubt, we are the first to benefit from authenticity, as it builds order and harmony in our beliefs and feelings. Authenticity thus reflects our purity of intention. For that reason, it helps us build trustworthy and lasting relationships with others.

Finally, **Integrity**, is the fit between motivation and action. It connects the motivation we derive from our purpose to our day-to-day actions. Integrity, as the "synthesis of virtues," is about living purpose in a natural, yet habitual way. It is earned over time and stimulates the ability to transform purpose into consistent action, performed on a regular basis, in harmony with our motivations. Integrity is the quality of being naturally authentic and coherent in every moment and in everything we do—both the most significant and the most commonplace.

Coherence, authenticity, and integrity represent the strength and quality of a purpose. We could say that they are the fundamental leading indicators, the "scorecard" for our personal purpose.

Living Our Purpose to the Fullest

For our purpose to develop, in its fullest sense, the three dimensions must be aligned. Purpose must be whole, of one piece. In this sense, our quest is not only to discover the *most inspiring* purpose, but also to achieve harmony

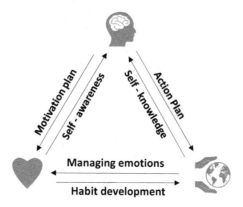

Fig. 8.3 Fundamental undertakings of purpose development (Graphic Design: Reproduced with permission from Freeland Communication Studio SL)

and fit between its three dimensions. To develop our purpose, and to live it out in a coherent, authentic, and integrated way, it is helpful to focus on six fundamental *areas of development*. Below, we briefly describe each one and include some reflective questions to illustrate their scope and development (Fig. 8.3).

1. Self-knowledge. Before all else, and for us to more fully understand our purpose, it is helpful to reflect upon our experiences, our talents and potential, and ask ourselves: in which areas of my work might I have the greatest impact on others? This type of knowledge comes from observation, analysis, and reflection upon our own activity as well as feedback from others. It is based on evidence, facts, results, and concrete behavior in action. This self-knowledge leads to the appreciation of what we do well—for having developed certain skills, strengths, or being gifted in certain ways in areas that we find meaningful. Focusing on what we do well can provide a sense of contribution to our identity.

Reflective questions to ask:

- What are my main talents and strengths? Have I identified them clearly?
- What am I especially good at? When do I function naturally, almost effortlessly, and it is valued, especially by others?
- How do my actions contribute to making the world a better place?
- In what activities do I feel I contribute my best self to others?

- Who are the beneficiaries of my work (people or groups)?
- What might my contribution be to the mission of my company/organization?

2. Self-awareness. In our journey to purpose, we will need to discover a higher level of awareness in ourselves and connect with our internal drivers—our beliefs, values, desires, dreams, feelings, affections, and so on. These help to provide us the guidance toward what may ultimately become our purpose. It is all about becoming aware of our deepest motivations, those which often remain invisible to others, and at times to ourselves as well, unless we take the time to sincerely reflect about them.

Reflective questions to ask:

- What are the problems in this world and in my professional environment that particularly concern me?
- What are three core values of most importance to me?
- What would I never accept, under any circumstance?
- What do I enjoy doing? What especially motivates me? What do I love about my work?
- What would I do if fear were not a consideration?
- Which past projects am I most proud of? What was at stake?
- In what activities do I feel a natural ability to give my best?
- The day I retire, what would I like people to say about the impact I had on them?

3. Motivation plan. This process is about reinforcing and enhancing the energy that drives our purpose. Through the motivation plan, the space occupied by our purpose in our inner dialogue—imagination, desires, values, affections, feelings, beliefs, and so on—is broadened. It enhances the motivational power of purpose and keeps it alive through actions such as reflection, meditation, visualization, storytelling, dialogue, and gratitude. Actions such as these can be distributed throughout our day or periodically concentrated into longer periods, in order to keep purpose front and center in our daily activities.

Reflective questions to ask:

- Do I recall my purpose and reflect on it every morning? Do I cherish it?
- Do I do this throughout the course of my day?
- Am I grateful for having a meaningful purpose?
- Do I take my purpose into consideration when making important decisions?

- What techniques or resources do I use to keep my purpose front of mind during the day?
- Do I have role models in my life who inspire and serve as an example to drive my purpose? Do I often communicate with people who have a similar purpose?
- Do I study topics related to my purpose that inspire and reinforce my commitment?

4. Action plan. Living our purpose means putting it into practice, defining it in personal commitments that are relevant, ambitious, meaningful, and thereby allowing it to lead us to act. The development of an action plan entails projects, actions, decisions, skill development, missions, objectives, and goals. Plans can be short term, lasting days or months, or on the other hand, they can cover a period of several years or even a lifetime.

Reflective questions to ask:

- How am I measuring progress relative to living my purpose? Do I have clear indicators to evaluate progress in my purpose?
- What can I change to make my purpose more effective?
- What new skills can I develop to make my purpose more effective?
- Who can I rely on to make my purpose more effective?
- What missions and SMART goals aligned with my purpose would I like to achieve in the coming days, months, or years?
- What stretch goal (ambitious or audacious) could I accomplish? How would I break it into actionable parts?

5. Habit development. Purpose is not only practiced in our plans but also, and especially, through our actions. Purpose is enacted when we develop habits, or spontaneous behaviors, that allow us to carry out our purpose in a natural way, often without effort and unconsciously. Good habits include, for example, the classic list of *virtues* (practical wisdom, justice, courage, and temperance) or the *seven habits* of S. Covey. These general frameworks, however, should be used with caution, because each purpose, depending on its content, will demand more unique or specific habits.

Reflective questions to ask:

- What do I do frequently and spontaneously throughout the day to live my purpose?
- Have I identified the main habits that drive or could drive my purpose?
- To what extent do I implement my purpose in my daily practice?

- What new habit(s) could I develop to accomplish my purpose with greater impact?
- What negative habits hold back the development of my purpose?

6. Managing emotions. The energy we derive from our purpose does not only come from reflection and meditation but also from our ability to connect our purposeful actions to our emotions and feelings. On the one hand, managing emotions is about identifying and enhancing the positive emotions that are generated when we live our purpose with integrity. On the other hand, it includes taming any of the negative emotions that might weaken our resolve. We can do this through techniques such as *reframing*, observation, and discernment.

Reflective questions to ask:

- How do I feel when I notice I am succeeding in furthering my purpose? What positive emotions does my purpose generate?
- Am I aware of these emotions in my daily practice? What do I do to enhance them?
- Do I celebrate my successes related to enacting my purpose?
- Do I keep a positive attitude in the face of difficulties? Do I look for ways to overcome "purpose failures" in a positive spirit?
- Am I able to enjoy the efforts I take in fulfilling my purpose?
- Do I find a sense of purpose in the little things in life, and overcoming monotony?
- What is my internal dialogue in difficult times or contradictions? At such times, does carrying out my purpose entail more of an effort?
- Am I positive about these difficulties and do I see them as opportunities to put my values into practice?

The Path of Purpose

Each process above plays an essential role in the development of purpose at work. The first two—self-knowledge and self-awareness—help us to discover our purpose and keep it real by adjusting to changes in our professional life as well as to the evolution and progress of our own abilities. The second two—motivation and action plan—help our purpose become a practical reality, leading and effectively directing our daily practice while feeding our need for satisfaction. And the final two—habit development and emotion management—help us live out our purpose over time in a natural and spontaneous way without having to think too much about it, while cherishing it at the same time. Together, these processes contribute to our living a full and meaningful purpose in life.

A good program for the development of purpose at work, one that is intentional about making a lasting impact, should pay balanced attention to all six processes, stimulating the unfolding of purpose in each. If one is omitted, there is a risk that the purpose will gradually lose strength and, over time, become lost. Many complain about a lack of effectiveness in the variety of personal growth and self-improvement programs that, despite being inspiring, do not achieve long-term changes in people. Perhaps the failure in those programs is that they concentrate on only one of the dimensions—head, heart, or hands—while all three are indispensable for a sustainable personal purpose.

In any case, a purposeful life is more than a goal to be perfectly attained or a particular destination, it is a way of living and being. We should not worry about whether or not we achieve *perfect* knowledge, *perfect* track record, or *perfect* motivation in our purpose as this may be a recipe for unhappiness and dissatisfaction. G.K. Chesterton's famous aphorism puts it well: "If a thing is worth doing, it is worth doing *badly*." What one should care most about then is always moving forward in one's purpose. It is a direction or journey more than a destination. This is where we find both a sense of real impact and a source of true contentment.

9

(Re)Discovering Organizational Purpose

Clara Fontán, Ángel Alloza, and Carlos Rey

We find ourselves immersed in a new economic and social cycle which we can name "the economy of intangibles".[1] This new economy is characterized by a growing share of intangible assets creating business value[2] and the fact that the perception of success is strongly associated with the recognition expressed by its various stakeholders (i.e. employees, clients, shareholders, suppliers and society in general). As we know, creating value is based on the equilibrium between an organization's capacity to sustain differentiation and the ability to achieve legitimization.[3] However, traditional analysis of the sources of differentiation and legitimization have changed: while in the past it was about creating new products and services, nowadays companies place value on the ability to manage intangible assets and resources, elements that form a more sustainable source of legitimacy[4] and are harder to copy.[5]

In this context, purpose emerges as an essential resource that is instrumental in achieving this uncopiable differentiation as well as securing stakeholder trust.[6] Indeed, recent studies point to the fact that performance of those companies that had a clear sense of purpose improved tenfold between 1996 and 2013 as compared to average performance demonstrated by S&P 500

C. Fontán (✉) • Á. Alloza
Corporate Excellence—Centre for Reputation Leadership, Madrid, Spain
e-mail: clara.fontan@corporateexcellence.org; angel.alloza@corporateexcellence.org

C. Rey
Universitat Internacional de Catalunya,
Barcelona, Spain
e-mail: carlosrey@uic.es

© The Author(s) 2019
C. Rey et al. (eds.), *Purpose-driven Organizations*,
https://doi.org/10.1007/978-3-030-17674-7_9

companies.[7] Generating an authentic and coherent purpose is fundamental for achieving organizational legitimacy and a good reputation.[8]

Today, citizens demand that organizations create ethical, social, environmental and economic value and thus have a positive impact on the quality and condition of people's lives. Think, for example, in the recent findings that demonstrate "an increase of between 17% and 33% of self-determination at work for a corporate objective focused on stakeholders compared to one focused on profits".[9] However, the gap between expectation and perception is currently very big: only 39% of citizens believe that organizations work hard to improve people's quality of life and they generally would not mind if 76% of brands disappeared.[10] In order to bridge this gap, a deep transformation in corporate leadership, culture and behavior is required. Many are asking CEOs and executives to rethink the role of their companies, their impact and the legacy they will leave for future generations.[11]

As we have seen in previous chapters, purpose is an organization's cornerstone. The role of purpose can be described as follows. Purpose...

- is the key conduit for generating unity throughout an organization;
- fosters leadership development at all levels of the organization;
- acts as a filter for making strategic decisions and establishing the fundamental principles that define the business model;
- provides an overarching framework for organizational agility, stimulating a joint combination of autonomy and alignment that liberates the highest potential in every employee;
- furnishes an organization with the meaning of its activity: the whys and wherefores of its actions, its place in the world and its understanding of its role as a relevant social actor.

In this chapter, we will tackle some fundamental questions for (re)discovering corporate purpose in an approach that integrates the external and internal perspectives of an organization. We will consider purpose as a process that is directed inside-out and is reinforced outside-in, generating connections and identity with different stakeholders. Finally, we will show that corporate purpose can be understood as a co-creation that results from a dynamic dialogue between key stakeholder groups.[12]

Although purpose seems to be a difficult aspect to define, it can always be found. Indeed, "we do not invent a higher purpose; it already exists".[13] Based on our research and experience, this process has to include at least four undertakings (see Fig. 9.1).

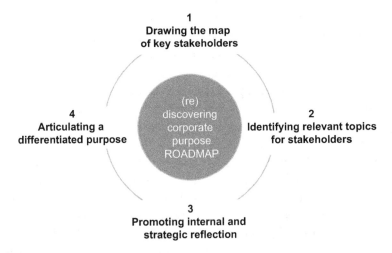

Fig. 9.1 A roadmap for (re)discovering corporate purpose

Drawing the Map of Key Stakeholders

From an internal perspective, employees have the frontline position to define the corporate purpose. And when setting purpose, companies offer their people an opportunity to participate in a project of superior order and to contribute something worthwhile,[14] appealing to their fundamental motivations as human beings; to their transcendent motivation.[15] That is why employees of companies with a strong sense of purpose play such an important role in the process of brand building. They are the first link to an organization's chain of relations.[16]

A good illustration of this is the case of Southwest Airlines. The true key to Southwest's business model and uniqueness resides in the construction of a solid corporate culture around a shared purpose: "connect people to what's important in their lives through friendly, reliable and low-cost air travel".[17] The company places its own employees at the center of its business model, convinced that their high commitment and satisfaction will translate into good quality service for its customers. As Southwest Airlines' Executive Director and CEO Gary Kelly says, "our people are our single greatest strength and most enduring long-term competitive advantage". Our principles that turn the company's corporate purpose into reality and serve as the basis for its values are a "warrior's spirit", "a servant's heart", and "a fun-living attitude". These three elements host the values that explain the Southwest living way.[18]

When it comes to defining corporate purpose, employees are key, but so are other stakeholders. Under the new logic of purpose, organizational purpose is created by cognitive, emotional and active connections to organizational purpose.[19] By expanding the traditional view of organizational boundaries beyond the traditional legal or competence perspectives, we incorporate a broader view, one based on identity.[20] In this view, other agents such as clients, shareholders, opinion leaders or experts, top managers or community members can be considered organizational members as much as they identify with the purpose of the organization.[21] Corporate purpose, rather than being defined *for* the stakeholders, is defined *with them*.[22]

Thus, when defining the purpose, companies should reflect upon the key stakeholders that ought to be part of the organization—those agents who are likely to identify with the organizational purpose. Identification and prioritization of these groups is driven by the degree of their potential identification with the organizational purpose and their ability to contribute to its development. An example of this process is found in the corporate purpose definition of BBVA: "Internally, the research exercise sought to identify the culture, values and expectations regarding the company. It explored the vision and values shared by the company's directors and staff at all company levels. Externally, it searched for market trends and stakeholder motivations, as well as direct and indirect competition. In total, BBVA interviewed 100,000 consumers in more than 20 countries. BBVA also undertook 100 focus groups with consumers, shareholders and employees, and 100 in-depth interviews with directors and opinion leaders".[23] Through this exercise, BBVA placed employees, clients, opinion leaders, shareholders, top management and society as key pieces of the stakeholder's map to define its purpose. But this is not a one-time project. Purpose definition is an ongoing process that evolves over time and is sensitive to internal and external contextual changes. And this is the case for BBVA.[24] Its identity (future) is stable over time, but the form of its purpose changed from the original form documented in 2003. At that time, BBVA articulated its purpose as "we work to create a better future for people", with the claim "going forward". Today it is defined as: "To bring the age of opportunity to everyone", with the claim "creating opportunities".

Identifying Relevant Topics for Stakeholders

Nowadays, expectations of an organization's role in society is much higher than in the past: today's citizens support companies for what they represent rather than for the products or services they sell.[25] They want companies that use their influence to have a positive impact on people's lives and to progress humankind. Creating a meaningful purpose requires not only an understanding of the issues that worry various stakeholders but also, to a certain extent, an ability to read trends and understand the logic of society. All in all, it means knowing which big social issues worry one's stakeholders and what the business is expected to do in order to improve this world.

Many companies use Sustainable Development Goals (SDG) as a reference point in the process of identifying their stakeholders' most relevant issues.[26] This domain incorporates such aspects as hunger, poverty, health, working conditions, consumption, climate and so on. Linking purpose with one of these universal values may be helpful in achieving strong identification with stakeholder groups.[27] Another referral point is what some call "paying attention to peripheries"[28] by looking at areas where people feel excluded and/or identifying social needs around the organization that have been disregarded or overlooked by society.

In order to identify relevant topics, companies must establish the means of actively listening to the agents that form the organization's stakeholder map. Their perceptions and opinions should be integrated with the analysis of relevant topics. For this, contextual, reputational and social intelligence is needed.[29] Keeping track of social trends and concerns allows organizations to identify truly relevant topics and narratives. A good example of introducing a system of corporate listening is provided by McDonalds, which used awareness of social concerns to re-focus its brand positioning in the face of a new global challenge, obesity. Another success story is the brand positioning performed by Dove[30] in the beginning of the 2000s around the concept of "true beauty". Dove decided to redefine its brand position, away from the mere idea of soap, to that which was more in line with the purpose of its corporate brand: create a better future every day. The starting point for positioning the brand around real or natural beauty was determined after studying the conclusions of international research showing that only 2% of women say that they consider themselves beautiful, and only 12% are satisfied with their physical appearance. The study also offered more specific data about social pressure reported by women, the result of more recent fashion and beauty trends. All of this gave rise to a campaign entitled: *For Real Beauty*. The campaign recognized a social concern and took a leading stance on the issue, placing the campaign as a specific narrative, generating socially relevant content aligned with corporate discourse that strengthened the company's stakeholder relations.[31]

Promoting Internal and Strategic Reflection

The analysis of relevant topics and monitoring of stakeholder opinions and expectations, which includes listening to employees, clients and society, have to be complemented by qualitative meetings among top management.

Executives must review this information and further engage in the critically important process of defining the organization's distinctive features—its legacy and the future it hopes to build. It does not mean that all companies have to "change the world". Instead, it means being able to commit to a shared belief, which leads a company to make a significant contribution in the areas where it operates.

Drawing on the *motivation—knowledge—action* dimensions of purpose that we reviewed in the previous chapters, an internal reflection of purpose can be seen as a striking balance between: (1) "want to be" for example, the corporate dream; (2) "have to be" for example, society and stakeholder expectations and (3) "can be" the company's objective capabilities and strengths. The "being" of the organization, found at the intersection of these three circles, is expressed through its purpose (see Fig. 9.2). An example of this relationship is found in Danone, which "wants to be" a company dedicated to health; "has to be" like this because of its consumer expectations, who trust the nutritional value of its products; and "can be" like this through its food production, which is the essence of its business model. The result is the important role that Danone plays in the development and well-being of all citizens in all parts of the world. The intersection of these three dimensions yields its reasons for existence, a purpose of superior order: creating a healthier future.

From a brand perspective, some authors recommend reflecting on purpose by analyzing relevant stakeholder topics in conjunction with the company's history and the impact its products and services might have in tackling such concerns.[32] In this way, purpose is reinforced by the company's historical legacy, its values and culture and its connection with consumer expectations.

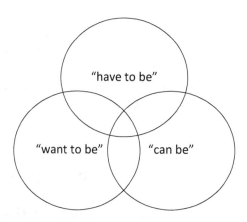

Fig. 9.2 Purpose as the intersection of three dimensions of 'being'

This turns the purpose on a central axis, sustaining the brand and its chosen direction.

Unilever offers a perfect example of this idea. In the last few years, the company has seen its brands, those that are defined around a purpose, double in economic growth as compared to brands that are not defined by purpose.[33] Some experts are now claiming this to be the way toward a different model of capitalism, in the long run, a conscious and humanistic capitalism.[34] In essence, purpose and the values that define it, worked to permeate the organization's leadership style, nudging Unilever to reword and redefine the positioning of all its brands. One of the most relevant projects that they are implementing is the *Sustainable Living Plan*, which attempts to significantly influence the behavior of employees (more than 170,000), suppliers (about 200,000), clients (2 million), partners and even competitors in order to help them choose and maintain a more sustainable way of life.[35]

Articulating a Differentiated Purpose

There is an irreplaceable imprint that characterizes a great purpose, one which has a positive and beneficial impact in the eyes of the audience.[36] A differentiating purpose must address a critical question: would our stakeholders miss us if we ceased to exist? As some experts suggest, "a great purpose is grounded in something universally true that is authentically delivered by your brand and product".[37] Think, for example, in the case of Patagonia. The organization was inspired by its founder's values and chose to place a social purpose at the center of its business: "tackle the environmental crisis". By doing this, the company managed to achieve a leading position in the market as a responsible, coherent organization, committed to the environment and generating social value.

Articulating a differentiated purpose is the most creative part of the process, because it implies distilling the corporate purpose to a sentence that can drive the corporate narrative and express the organization's unique contribution to the world.[38] Corporate branding experts recommend[39]: (1) be concise by using short phrases, (2) be straightforward by avoiding jargon, (3) seek what is characteristic—"this is us", (4) stay authentic, firmly ingrained in the organization and (5) seek what is timeless, rooted in the past and forward looking to the future. That, for example, is the purpose of Walt Disney, which has been guiding the company for decades: "create happiness by providing the finest in entertainment for people of all ages, everywhere".[40] Or Nestlé's purpose, reflected in three overarching ambitions: Enable healthier and happier lives (focusing on nutrition, water and rural development); develop thriving, resilient communities (focusing on sustainability); and steward resources for future generations (with a focus on having zero environmental impact in operations).[41]

Besides, purpose must reach, not only employees, but also the other stakeholders of the company. As some experts suggest, purpose must be "clear enough that the investors, employees, partners, and customers could articulate it".[42] It can be compared to a song. From the official version, different players can make covers in different styles (pop, rock, heavy, unplugged, symphonic orchestra etc.) but "the key is for everyone to follow the same melody".[43] Thus, purpose must be expressed in a way that can be used and replicated by different stakeholders without losing its essence. Examples can be seen with Starbucks: "to inspire and nurture the human spirit—one person, one cup and one neighborhood at a time"; or Facebook: "to share and make the world more open and connected".

Finally, purpose must be expressed in a way that favors co-creation with those who are expected to identify with the purpose. Fostering purpose cocreation requires that its articulation invites key stakeholders to become a part of the purpose by participating in the formation of its definition and meaning. Thus, the way purpose is articulated has to impel customers, employees, suppliers and so on, not only to be beneficiaries of the purpose but also cocreators of the same. It has to reflect the aforementioned idea that purpose is not made *for* the stakeholders but *with them*. The company's purpose is created by internalization and it is reinforced by identification, which occurs when stakeholders groups identify with it. A good example of this might be the purpose of Nike—"to bring inspiration and innovation to every athlete in the world". In the articulation of its purpose, Nike actively encourages customers (athletes) to inspire each other, offering a narrative—"just do it"—that goes far beyond the products Nike sells.[44]

Once purpose is defined, it has to permeate not only the corporate narrative but also the production of the company's content, brand experience and messaging. However, many organizations fail from this perspective. Indeed, not all companies that have a purpose are recognized by their purpose. Being true to purpose is a necessary condition, but being recognized by purpose requires a joint development of internal and external communications.[45] Think, for example, in the case of TOMS, whose marketing claim "one for one" promise to deliver a pair of free shoes to a child in need for every sale of their retail product, or Patagonia, whose advertising campaign "Don't buy this jacket" promotes responsible consumption and reinforces the articulation of their purpose; or Zappos, through the values and corporate culture expressed in the "delivering happiness" purpose. This approach requires consolidating the corporate brand as the platform for expressing purpose. Thus, the purpose turns into an extremely important tool: the central axis of corporate narrative strategy as well as a platform for relations with stakeholders.

In this chapter, we have discussed how to discover and rediscover a corporate purpose in a way that creates connections between the organization and its stakeholders. We have suggested a roadmap for setting a relevant purpose, aiming to generate an authentic connection with stakeholder groups and mobilize them into supportive behaviors.

Notes

1. Carreras, E., Alloza, A., & Carreras, A. (2013). The economy of intangibles and reputation. In *Corporate reputation* (pp. 19–32). Madrid: LID Editorial Empresarial.
2. Hall, R. (1992). The strategic analysis of intangible resources. *Strategic Management Journal, 13*(2), 135–144.
3. Suchman, M. (1995). Managing legitimacy: Strategic and institutional approaches. *The Academy of Management Review, 20*(3), 571–610.
4. Scherer, A. G., Palazzo, G., & Seidl, D. (2013). Managing legitimacy in complex and heterogeneous environments: Sustainable development in a globalized world. *Journal of Management Studies, 50*(2), 259–284.
5. Hall, R. (1992). The strategic analysis of intangible resources. *Strategic Management Journal, 13*(2), 135–144.
6. Sisodia, R. (2016). Four tenets to fix capitalism & unlock your business's potential. *IESE Insight, 31*(31).
7. Mackey, J., & Sisodia, R. (2013). *Conscious capitalism. Liberating the heroic spirit of business.* Cambridge: Harvard Business Review Press.
8. Carreras, E., Alloza, A., & Carreras, A. (2013). *Corporate reputation.* Madrid: LID Editorial Empresarial.
9. Parmar, B. L., Keevil, A., & Wicks, A. C. (2019). People and profits: The impact of corporate objectives on employees' need satisfaction at work. *Journal of Business Ethics, 154*(1), 13.
10. Havas Group. (2017). Meaningful brands 2017. Retrieved December 10, 2018, from https://www.meaningful-brands.com/en
11. Canals, J. (2014). Global leadership development, strategic alignment and CEOs commitment. *Journal of Management Development, 33*(5), 487–502; Raelin, J. (2015). Rethinking leadership. *MIT Sloan Management Review, 56*(4), 95–96.
12. Hatch, M. J., & Schultz, M. (2010). Towards a theory of brand co-creation with implications for brand governance. *Journal of Brand Management, 17*(8), 590–604.

13. Quinn, R. E., & Thakor, A. V. (2018, July–August). Creating a purpose-driven organization. *Harvard Business Review*, 78–85.
14. Bailey, C., & Madden, A. (2016). What makes work meaningful-or meaningless? *MIT Sloan Management Review, 57*(4).
15. Cardona, P., & Rey, C. (2008). *Management by missions.* New York: Palgrave Macmillan.
16. Saleem, F., & Iglesias, O. (2016). Mapping the domain of the fragmented field of internal branding. *Journal of Product & Brand Management, 25*(1), 43–57.
17. Southwest Airlines' purpose. Retrieved December 17, 2018, from https://www.swabiz.com/html/about-southwest/index.html?int=GNAVABOU TSWA_SBIZ
18. Thomas, M. (2015). Strategic principles at southwest airlines. *Strategic Direction, 31*(8), 10–12.
19. Rey, C., & Bastons, M. (2018). Three dimensions of effective mission implementation. *Long Range Planning, 51*(4), 580–585.
20. Santos, F. M., & Eisenhardt, K. M. (2005). Organizational boundaries and theories of organization. *Organization Science, 16*(5), 491–508.
21. Pérez López, J. A. (2014). *Foundations of management.* Madrid: Rialp.
22. Ind, N., Iglesias, O., & Schultz, M. (2013). Building brands together: Emergence and outcomes of co-creation. *California Management Review, 55*(3), 5–26.
23. Alloza, A. (2008). Brand engagement and brand experience at BBVA, the transformation of a 150 years old company. *Corporate Reputation Review, 11*(4).
24. Ibid.
25. Hollensbe, E., Wookey, C., Hickey, L., George, G., & Nichols, C. V. (2014). Organizations with purpose. *Academy of Management Journal, 57*(5), 1227–1234.
26. Mirvis, P., Googins, B., & Kinnicutt, S. (2010). Vision, mission, values: Guideposts to sustainability. *Organizational Dynamics, 39*(4), 316–324.
27. Stengel, J. (2012). *Grow: How ideals power growth and profit at the world's greatest companies.* New York: Crown Business.
28. Almandoz, J., Lee, Y., & Ribera, A. (2018). Unleashing the power of purpose: 5 steps to transform your business, *IESE Insight, 37*, Second Quarter, 44–51.
29. Gregory, A., & Halff, G. (2017). Understanding public relations in the 'sharing economy'. *Public Relations Review, 43*(1).
30. Jevons, C., Buil, I., Merrilees, B., & De Chernatony, L. (2013). Introduction: Thought leadership in brand management. *Journal of Business Research, 66*(1), 1–3.
31. Bissell, K., & Rask, A. (2010). Real women on real beauty: Self-discrepancy, internalization of the thin ideal, and perceptions of attractiveness and thin-

ness in Dove's Campaign for Real Beauty. *International Journal of Advertising, 29*(4), 643–668.

32. Rodríguez Vilá, O., & Bharadwaj, S. (2017). Competing on social purpose. Brands that win by tying mission to growth. *Harvard Business Review*, 94–101.

33. Ind, N., & Horlings, S. (Eds.) (2016). *Brands with a conscience: How to build a successful and responsible brand*. London: Kogan Page Publishers.

34. Ibidem.

35. Retrieved December 16, 2018, from https://www.unilever.com/sustainable-living/our-sustainable-living-report-hub/

36. Birkinshaw, J., Foss, N. J., & Lindenberg, S. (2014). Combining purpose with profits. *MIT Sloan Management Review, 55*(3), 49.

37. Bonchek, M., & France, C. (2018). How marketers can connect profit and purpose. *Harvard Business Review Digital Articles*, 2–5.

38. Flory, M., & Iglesias, O. (2010). Once upon a time: The role of rhetoric and narratives in management research and practice. *Journal of Organizational Change Management, 23*(2), 113–119.

39. Greyser, S. A., & Urde, M. (2019). What does your corporate brand stand for? *Harvard Business Review, 97*(1), 80–88.

40. Trevor, J., & Varcoe, B. (2017). How aligned is your organization? *Harvard Business Review Digital Articles*, 2–6.

41. Chevreux, L., Lopez, J., & Mesnard, X. (2017). The best companies know how to balance strategy and purpose. *Harvard Business Review Digital Articles*, 2–5.

42. Trevor, J., & Varcoe, B. (2017). How aligned is your organization? *Harvard Business Review Digital Articles*, 2–6.

43. Greyser, S. A., & Urde, M. (2019). What does your corporate brand stand for? *Harvard Business Review, 97*(1), 80–88.

44. Bonchek, M. (2016). How to build a strategic narrative. *Harvard Business Review Digital Articles*, 2–4.

45. Rodríguez Vilá, O., & Bharadwaj, S. (2017). Competing on social purpose. Brands that win by tying mission to growth. *Harvard Business Review*, 94–101.

10

Measuring the Purpose Strength

Alvaro Lleo, Carlos Rey, and Nuria Chinchilla

In the preceding chapters, a new logic for the twenty-first-century organization was proposed—the logic of leading based on a shared and common business purpose, one that captures the mind, captivates the heart, and guides the day-to-day routines of every individual in the organization. In view of this new logic, though, the question becomes, how are leaders to assess whether or not the purpose of the business is truly common and deeply shared?

To be able to answer such questions, it is crucial we have a perspective that allows for the gathering of our employees' thoughts and feelings, a system that assesses the organization's health, and its areas for improvement upon which to base our actions. These actions will be the more effective the better the assessment systems in which we make our diagnosis. It is not only about measuring discreet variables, but also knowing how they are related to each other,

A. Lleo (✉)
University of Navarra, TECNUN School of Engineering,
San Sebastian, Spain
e-mail: alleo@tecnun.es

C. Rey
Universitat Internacional de Catalunya,
Barcelona, Spain
e-mail: carlosrey@uic.es

N. Chinchilla
IESE Business School, University of Navarra,
Barcelona, Spain
e-mail: chinchilla@iese.edu

© The Author(s) 2019
C. Rey et al. (eds.), *Purpose-driven Organizations*,
https://doi.org/10.1007/978-3-030-17674-7_10

PURPOSE STRENGTH MODEL

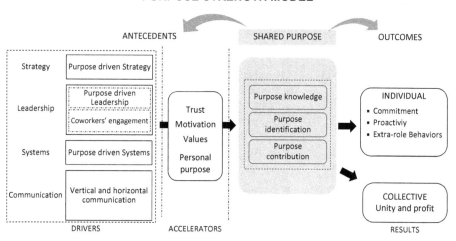

Fig. 10.1 The Purpose Strength Model

identifying the causes of some of them, the effects of others, and which variables accelerate the relationships among them.

In order to meet this threefold objective of assessing, diagnosing and enhancing the purpose strength in an organization, we developed the Purpose Strength Model, shown in Fig. 10.1, which establishes the basis for the development of a measuring tool.

We begin by focusing on the core of the new paradigm (shown in the middle of the diagram below), the shared purpose. Based on this paradigm, we then integrate those remaining variables that play a significant role. We will firstly identify the main consequences. We further identify the main antecedents on which it is possible to act in order to design an organization around a shared purpose (drivers) and, also, the variables that speed up or slow its development (accelerators).

Shared Purpose as the Core

The essence of the model we propose lies in the generation of a shared and common business purpose, one that pivots on a triad of knowledge, motivation, and action.[1] In other words, for a business purpose to be shared, it must be such that it illuminates the mind (knowledge), captivates the heart (motivation), and guides the daily work of the organization's employees (action): illuminating, captivating, and guiding are the three elements that must characterize the business purpose so that it becomes internalized by all (Fig. 10.2).

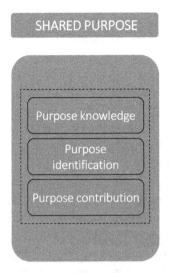

Fig. 10.2 Shared purpose and its dimensions

However, it must be recalled that the generation of this shared purpose is a lengthy, continuous process and, at times, an unstable equilibrium.

It is a lengthy process because purpose is not something one should define from a top-down view and expect others to internalize immediately. All too often, organizations have a very well-defined purpose that is announced clearly and yet, at the same time, we often still encounter many within teams who hardly identify with it. *Identification* is a key word. Organizational purpose and the manner in which it is generated are quite important. The existence of sincere dialogue within the team achieves a climate of trust and helps people open up and share their individual purposes. This is vital in building common purpose—a purpose that comes to be shared by everyone.

But, how well do we know the individual purposes of the people who work in our organization? Do we provide them space, so that they can think about and define their individual purpose? Once done, do we respect and acknowledge that purpose? Do we create environments where people feel comfortable and share their purpose? And do managers lead the way by sharing their own purpose? Certainly, answering such questions requires significant time, not to mention enough serenity to even raise them. For this reason, the process takes time. Consider this "the cost." The advantage? It is quite clear: as the organization invests time in the generation of shared purpose, the door will open for team members to identify with the purpose and assume it as their own, thereby increasing commitments throughout the organization.

Yet, it is important to remember that the creation and connection of purpose is a continuous process. Endless, one might say. There are at least two reasons for this: first, because circumstances change and just as the organization needs to continually adapt to the environment, the purpose must also adapt to these new circumstances. This is not to say that an organization's purpose is like a weather vane. What it means, however, is that as the environment evolves, it will require that organizations adapt and revalidate to ensure that their purpose relates to new market demands. Second, shifts in personnel bring new staff to teams. With the integration of new team members, maintaining an ongoing dialogue becomes increasingly important so that purpose remains common and shared.

Finally, shared purpose, its creation and proliferation, can be an unstable equilibrium. This becomes most notable when trying to manage the balance between employees' day-to-day requirements and their sense of purpose. Running the business from a genuine perspective of purpose requires a balance between the short and long view. The patience required for purpose and the pressure demanded by results drives a wedge that creates tension: if we focus only on the day-to-day routine, we distance ourselves from the purpose and if we focus only on purpose, sometimes we risk losing sight of the short-term business requirements. This tension necessitates knowing how to manage this instability, such that we live our everyday life with a sense of purpose, yet live our purpose with a sense of everyday life.

For these reasons, it is especially important to have tools for measuring and assessing the degree to which the organization is purpose-oriented, as intuition does not always go hand-in-hand with reality. It happens rather often that upon measuring, managers are amazed to find their efforts are not producing the expected results or, even worse, they are actually regressing. Of course, it also happens that some managers are pleasantly surprised to see their efforts yielding better results than expected. Maintaining a high level of purpose (something that should be natural in all organizations) requires taking the pulse of the organization frequently, without ever letting down one's guard. The more we are able to bring shared purpose into our sphere of work, the greater will be the effects and consequences for organizations.

Consequences of Having a Shared Purpose

From the perspective of the individual in the organization, we can distinguish at least three consequences of having a shared purpose: it increases commitment, proactivity, and extra-role behaviors (Fig. 10.3).

Several authors assert that commitment, first and foremost, expresses the link established between the person and the organization.[2] More specifically,

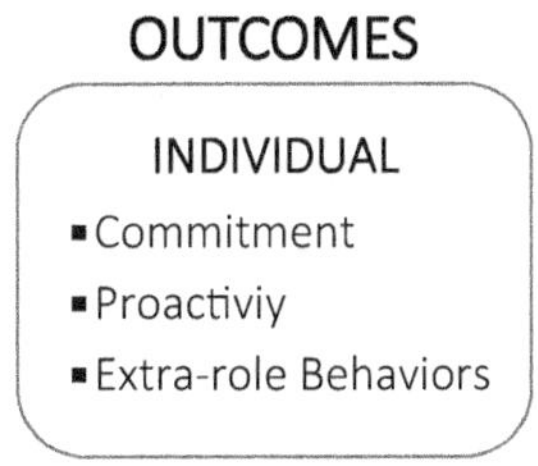

OUTCOMES

INDIVIDUAL
- Commitment
- Proactiviy
- Extra-role Behaviors

Fig. 10.3 Individual outcomes of having a shared purpose

that shared purpose generates what is called affective commitment,[3] that is, the emotional bond that causes employees to stay in an organization because it feels like their own. There are also numerous studies that relate affective commitment to a decrease in rotation and absenteeism,[4] an increase in employee satisfaction,[5] as well as an increase in productivity and organizational performance.[6]

While commitment is a connection, proactivity is a disposition—an attitude of wanting to contribute to the organization's goals.[7] In this case, employees feel a certain ownership, and also wish to contribute to advancing the shared purpose because they identify with it.

Finally, the third individual-level consequence is the generation of extra-role behaviors.[8] That is the phenomenon in which employees willingly take on more than is required. It is a clear indication that people identify with the organization's purpose as their own. But when purpose fails to change behaviors or express itself in concrete ways, it is neither as shared nor as internalized as had been thought.[9]

In addition to individual consequences, shared purpose has consequences that impact the organization at a collective level. Some authors have stressed the importance of measuring the impact of purpose on a Unity-Profit[10] curve. "Unity" is the variable that measures the degree to which company members identify with a given purpose, and "Profit" is understood as the company's economic result. As shown by previous research, these two variables are not by themselves orthogonal, but, when analyzed together, they allow us to see what type of organization we are generating.[11] For example, the organization with an effective purpose will result in high levels of the two variables and often exhibit extraordinary culture, compared to organizations that have only high levels of unity (paternalistic cultures), or only seek profitability (aggressive cultures), or low levels of both (bureaucratic cultures) (Fig. 10.4).

In light of such positive consequences resulting from the creation of shared purpose, we may ask ourselves, how best to achieve it? What tools can we deploy to enhance our purpose strength?

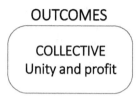

OUTCOMES

COLLECTIVE
Unity and profit

Fig. 10.4 Collective outcomes of having a shared response

Antecedents of Shared Purpose

In order to best structure an organization from a perspective of purpose, it is important to understand the logic that governs this process. We believe that the metaphor of the gardener describes it best. How do you grow a plant? Certainly not by stretching it, for if you do, it may damage the stem and perish. The art of gardening consists of creating and sustaining a suitable environment so that the plant can grow robustly. This concept applies to organizations and their design as well. Just as the gardener selects, waters, and fertilizes the land, we must work the organizational drivers within our control.

However, one should not expect that by simply managing these drivers will result in an immediate effect. What can be expected is the generation of a working environment where people become increasingly aware of their role in the bigger picture, which in turn helps the purpose become more common and shared by everyone. These are the levers to be pulled. There are, at least, four key organizational levers on which we can act to design a purpose-oriented organization: strategy, systems, leadership, and communication (Fig. 10.5).

Strategy marks the way forward, but the real goal here lies in defining the strategy in such a way that unambiguously points the organization toward its stated purpose. This can be reinforced through the use of purpose-oriented objectives that make the strategy real and relatable to the purpose. It has been said that "purpose without objectives is a dead purpose. Likewise, objectives without purpose are blind objectives."[12] Purpose will not only help to provide a reason for working every day, but it also prioritizes our work putting emphasis and energy on those objectives that answer the company's call. From this perspective, strategy will be more coherent and authentic to the extent that it helps put into practice the organization's purpose.

The systems of a company are its policies and procedures, those that guide its people in their day-to-day work and move them down the path set out by its strategy. One of the aims of a management system should be to ensure that the organization's purpose is noticed, and becomes part of and gives meaning

ANTECEDENTS

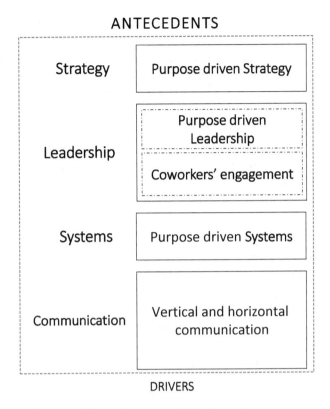

Fig. 10.5 Organizational drivers that precede the shared purpose generation

to daily work. The whole point about this is that "purpose" makes no difference, unless it changes the way people operate or the way they do business.[13] Recruitment, training and development, task planning, performance evaluation, incentive systems, budget management, and the rest of the company's policies should be focused on developing and enhancing the shared and common purpose. Otherwise, purpose becomes nothing but a slogan that appears on the website, appealed to in official speeches, but not very fertile as it lacks presence in people's day-to-day reality. The core of any management system is that it drives the dynamics of the organization and that it has an impact on the employees' daily activities to the point that employees might say: "I'm not here simply to achieve some objectives; instead, my work is oriented towards achieving the company's shared purpose."

Leadership is another major driver of shared purpose. A purpose-oriented organization requires leadership capable of reaching the hearts and minds of co-workers by generating an understanding that working for the common purpose is worthwhile.[14] Two types of leadership can be distinguished. On the one hand, there are managers and executives who promote the purpose, leading by example. This is recognized by co-workers and employees as authentic and coherent. Real leaders succeed in getting their people to strongly accept their words yet freely adhere to the organizational purpose. Recognizing and valuing the differences of each person within the organization, generating work teams in which cooperation takes precedence over competition, promoting co-creation, continuously appealing to the common purpose as the main motivating reason for day-to-day work, and delegating responsibility so that workers assume the mission of furthering the purpose—all are actions that depend on the organization's leadership capacity. On the other hand, it is equally important that there exists a form of shared leadership: the kind of leadership that is exercised at all company levels and in all of its areas, in which co-workers mutually reinforce the transmission and identification with the organization's purpose.[15]

Finally, consistent communication is a fundamental tool for transmitting organizational purpose in such a way that illuminates and fascinates all involved. Considering this as a driver, organizations must ensure the appropriate channels exist to, not only transmit the message, but also to show that decisions are justifiably based upon it. One of the design challenges is that organizations should be able to capture communication upwards. The key is to be able to grasp organizations' feelings and thoughts and, in turn, promote purpose as part of an overall internal dialogue.

Measuring these four variables—strategy, systems, leadership, and communication—will allow leaders to understand the extent to which the company is properly managing those organizational levers that promote a shared purpose.

Accelerators (or Decelerators) That Impact Shared Purpose

Accelerators, or decelerators, are aspects that either positively or negatively impact the influence the drivers have on specific people within the organization. They must be understood and taken into account because they play a role in the effectiveness of the antecedents of purpose. Likewise, understanding and knowing how best to boost the drivers will make them more impactful (Fig. 10.6).

There are four determining factors that should be considered: trust between managers and workers, values held by team members, their motivations, and each employee's purpose.

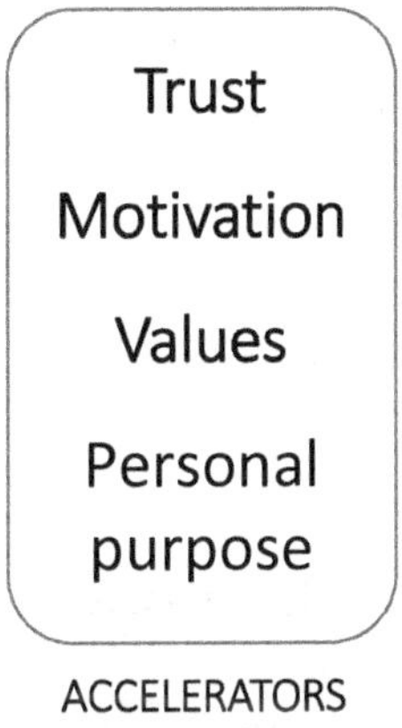

> Trust
>
> Motivation
>
> Values
>
> Personal purpose

ACCELERATORS

Fig. 10.6 Accelerators (or decelerators) of shared purpose generation

Some authors define trust as the decision to make oneself vulnerable to another person by assuming the risk of depending on that other person.[16] Being vulnerable allows for more authentic and stronger relationships.[17] Showing that we have made a mistake, opening up to others, sharing the aspects that are important to us, what motivates us, or our personal purpose, are evidence of making ourselves vulnerable.[18] In this way, trust determines the relationship between the background and the creation of a shared purpose because, so long as there is trust, the resulting work environment will provide psychological safety,[19] making it easier for people to open up and show themselves as they truly are. The generation of trust will facilitate getting to know the real person behind each character,[20] to know and recognize their uniqueness and to treat them in a more authentic way.

Values and motivation express the deepest aspects of people, the ideals that govern their behavior, and the motives that drive them to act. We adhere to the proposals of authors who identify four types of values among an organization's employees: increasing economic benefits, creating a comfortable relationship environment, developing personally and professionally, and ultimately contributing to the larger society.[21] Pérez-López identified three types of motives[22]: extrinsic ones, or what is received from outside (salary, recognition, fame, etc.), intrinsic ones, or what is acquired (learning, satisfaction, competences, virtues, etc.), and, finally, transcendent ones, or that which is given to others (service, caring, etc.). People's values and motives will influence the creation of the shared purpose. Thus, for example, it will be easier to generate a shared purpose with people who have transcendent motives and among whom contribution values prevail, rather than with others whose motives are primarily extrinsic or intrinsic.[23]

Finally, each employee's personal purpose will also influence the generation of common and shared purpose.[24] Having invested time in searching for, reflecting on and defining a personal purpose, one that gives meaning to day-to-day life, makes it easier to share as well as to analyze the extent to which the organization's purpose encompasses the personal one. The more meaning and purpose, the easier it will be for people to share and identify with the organization's common purpose.

Assessing in Order to Be Able to Improve

In this chapter, based on our experience and research, we have outlined the components of our Purpose Strength Model (see Fig. 10.1): a model that shows how certain variables are articulated around a shared purpose and establishes the basis for the development of a diagnostic tool.

From this model, having reliable and validated questionnaires for measuring the variables of the model will allow us to assess and to take to the pulse of an organization. These evaluations will allow us to be aware of the degree to which an organization has a purpose that gives meaning and guides day-to-day activities. Moreover, statistical analysis can help us to understand how the variables are related between themselves and to establish concrete plans that help boost it, measuring the progress and impact that the implemented actions have on the organization over time.

We do not consider this proposal to be a closed model. Future research will allow us to expand its scope and depth by including new variables, such as taking into account the purpose of other stakeholders, customer satisfaction, favorable purchasing attitudes, and the reputation or the relevance of the corporate brand.

That future research may indicate adjustments to our model does not dissuade us; indeed, this idea fascinates us. The ability to expand the frontiers of knowledge on how to generate inspiring organizations drives us. This is our goal: to deepen our understanding of the dynamics of developing purpose-driven organizations, to generate practical tools that make this a reality, and to help companies generate more sustainable work environments that combine unity and profit.

Notes

1. Rey, C., & Bastons, M. (2018). Three dimensions of effective mission implementation. *Long Range Planning, 51*(4), 580–585.

2. Meyer, J. P. (2016). *Handbook of employee commitment*. Northampton, MA: Edward Elgar Publishing.
3. Lofquist, E. A., Isaksen, S. G., & Dahl, T. J. (2018). Something fishy: Exploring change, job engagement and work environment in the Norwegian Directorate of Fisheries. *Journal of Change Management, 18*(4), 1–23.
4. Mathieu, J. E., & Zajac, D. M. (1990). A review and meta-analysis of the antecedents, correlates, and consequences of organizational commitment. *Psychological Bulletin, 108*(2), 171–194.
5. Meyer, J. P., Allen, N. J., & Smith, C. A. (1993). Commitment to organizations and occupations: Extension and test of a three-component conceptualization. *Journal of Applied Psychology, 78*(538), 538–551.
6. Dayan, M. (2010). Managerial trust and NPD team performance: Team commitment and longevity as mediators. *Journal of Business & Industrial Marketing, 25*(2), 94–105.
7. Griffin, M. A., Neal, A., & Parker, S. K. (2007). A new model of work role performance: Positive behavior in uncertain and interdependent contexts. *Academy of Management Journal, 50*(2), 327–347.
8. Motowidlo, S. J. (2000). Some basic issues related to contextual performance and organizational citizenship behavior in human resource management. *Human Resource Management Review, 10*(1), 115–126.
9. Lofquist, E. A., Isaksen, S. G., & Dahl, T. J. (2018). Something fishy: Exploring change, job engagement and work environment in the Norwegian Directorate of Fisheries. *Journal of Change Management, 18*(4), 1–23.
10. Cardona, P. & Rey, C. (2008). *Management by missions*. New York: Palgrave Macmillan.
11. Kotter, J. P. (2008). *Corporate culture and performance*. New York: Simon & Schuster.
12. Cardona, P., & Rey, C. (2008). *Management by missions*. New York: Palgrave Macmillan.
13. White, A., Yakis-Douglas, B., Helanummi-Cole, H., & Ventresca, M. (2017). Purpose-led organization: "Saint Antony" reflects on the idea of organizational purpose, in principle and practice. *Journal of Management Inquiry, 26*(1), 101–107.
14. Marimón, F., Mas-Machuca, M., & Rey, C. (2016). Assessing the internalization of the mission. *Industrial Management & Data Systems, 116*(1), 170–187.
15. Cardona, P., & Rey, C. (2009). El liderazgo centrado en la misión. *Harvard Deusto Business Review, 180*, 46–56.
16. Mayer, R. C., Davis, J. H., & Schoorman, F. D. (1995). An integrative model of organizational trust. *Academy of Management Review, 20*(3), 709–734.
17. Brown, B. (2012). *The power of vulnerability*. Louisville, CO: Sounds True.
18. Lleó de Nalda, A., Guillén, M., & Gil Pechuan, I. (2016). The influence of ability, benevolence, and integrity in trust between managers and subordi-

nates: The role of ethical reasoning. *Business Ethics: A European Review, 25*(4), 556–576.

19. Edmondson, A. C. (2018). *The fearless organization: Creating psychological safety in the workplace for learning, innovation, and growth.* Hoboken, NJ: Wiley.

20. Guillén, M., Lleó de Nalda, A., & Marco Perles, G. (2011). Towards a more humanistic understanding of organizational trust. *Journal of Management Development, 30*(6), 605–614.

21. Malbašić, I., Rey, C., & Potočan, V. (2015). Balanced organizational values: From theory to practice. *Journal of Business Ethics, 130*(2), 437–446.

22. Pérez López, J. A. (2014). *Foundations of management.* Madrid: Rialp.

23. Chinchilla, N., Jiménez, E., & García-Lombardía, P. (2018, April 16). *Integrar la vida: Liderar con éxito la trayectoria profesional y personal en un mundo global.* Editorial Ariel.

24. Hanson, J. A., & VanderWeele, T. J. (2019). *The comprehensive measure of meaning.* Harvard University Technical Report.

Epilogue

Carlos Rey

When I was a child, I admired those who were in business. From the glamorous to the mundane, I loved how companies did so many good things for people. They made movies and videogames but also cars, highways, furniture, clothing, toys, and so on. I thought companies that provided such essential products and services should be very interesting places to play a part in creating a better society. Years after, I enrolled in business administration studies but what I encountered was profoundly disappointing. Everything I learned was about statistics and theories regarding market forces, profitability, competitiveness, productivity, money, and power. In this world, people were merely resources, objects, regarded all too often as fungible.

One day, my professor of strategy wrote a quote on the blackboard that made a lasting impression on me. It was from a Nobel Prize economist and it said: "The only purpose of a company is to maximize shareholder profit." Outraged, I raised my hand and said: "Do you really think I am going to dedicate my professional life solely to make money for shareholders?" He responded indignantly, "you must be a communist!" To which I replied: "No, I am not a communist, but I think I have made the wrong career choice!"

A few months later I graduated and decided to forget all about the business world. I was deeply upset with myself, thinking that I had wasted the last few years of my life studying things that had nothing to do with me. I felt completely lost.

I grabbed a backpack and headed off to India.

© The Author(s) 2019
C. Rey et al. (eds.), *Purpose-driven Organizations*,
https://doi.org/10.1007/978-3-030-17674-7

Shortly after arriving, I located a Tibetan refugee camp where I stayed and became friends with a Buddhist monk. We spent long hours meditating and chatting about our inner self. I traveled through India, rode elephants, visited villages and towns, and temples of many religions and tribes. I was filling my backpack with unique experiences full of life.

One day, while chatting on the meaning of life with a National Geographic journalist, I learned of Kalighat, a Hindu temple in the city of Calcutta dedicated to Kali, the goddess of death. Years ago, the temple was donated to the Missionaries of Charity and, since then, it had become a home for the homeless and terminally ill. My friend encouraged me to visit Kalighat and said: "if you want to understand the meaning of life, you must first face the meaning of death."

Two days later I got on a train to Calcutta. When I arrived at the house of the Missionaries of Charity, I found the nuns silently meditating in the chapel. I stayed outside, peeking in to not disturb them. One of the nuns who was sitting on the floor near the door gestured for me to sit next to her. I went in and sat down. When I looked closely, I could not believe my eyes. Do you know who it was? Mother Teresa of Calcutta!

It was a moment that's hard to put into words. Needless to say, I never imagined I would even get to see her. And there I was, sitting silently by one of the most admired people in the world. At the end of the meditation session, Mother took me onto the patio next to the chapel and after some conversation, I said to her: "Mother, I want to go to Kalighat." She looked at me profoundly with an expression that is hard to describe and said: "You can go to Kalighat but every morning before leaving, you must come here and do an hour of meditation." She was so right.

When I arrived in Kalighat I was asked to take care of an infirmed Hindu man who had not had a family or a roof over his head his entire life. They said to me: "You will be his family, his father, his mother, his brother." And so that is what I became. Every day I meditated with Mother Teresa for an hour and the rest of the day I spent my time caring for the Hindu man. I washed him, I fed him, I cut his hair and nails, I recited Hindu verses to him, and I sang songs to him, but most of the time I just sat next to him holding his hand. They were unforgettable days in which I, paradoxically, felt extremely happy.

Until finally, fate struck. The man whom I had come to love like a brother died in my arms. I felt my soul crying out. All the injustice of the world was upon me. Nothing made sense. After three months in India, where I came to find meaning, I felt like I had found none at all. That night, I lay awake searching for answers.

The next morning, I sat next to Mother for meditation, but I was devastated. Even with the best meditation techniques from my friend, the Buddhist monk, I could not stay focused.

At the end of the hour of silence, Mother Teresa, as though she had read my mind, invited me again onto the patio next to the chapel. It was only five or so minutes, but her message has stayed with me forever: "Put love into everything you do."

That was the end of my trip. That day I came to understand with an extraordinary clarity that everything I had studied about market forces, competitiveness, profit, power, those things I had once dismissed, now had a very different meaning to me. That phrase, which came from the lips of the most humble person, who spent her life working for the poorest of the poor, is the essence of everything written in this book. For it describes the golden rule of becoming a purpose-driven organization: No matter what you do, make sure to put love into everything you do.

Index[1]

A

Accelerators, 120, 126–128
Action plan, 36, 104, 105
Adaptability, 76, 82, 83
Agile purpose, 75–84
Aigües de Barcelona, 36, 38
Alignment, 10, 11, 51, 52, 58,
  79–81, 83, 92, 108
Alpha Omega, 24, 81, 93
Amazon, 11
Analytical logic, 45, 49, 52
Apple, 31, 32
Authenticity, 68, 90, 100–101

B

Barclay's, 7
BBVA, 110
Ben & Jerry's, 66, 67
Bimbo, 90
Biok, 81, 93
BlackRock, 48

Brand purpose, 50
Business model, 7, 44–47, 49–52,
  56n43, 56n47, 108, 109,
  112

C

Coherence, 12, 92, 100–101
Communication, 9, 21, 24, 58,
  81, 88–94, 114, 124,
  126
Competences, 6, 59, 62, 63, 77, 80,
  110, 127
Core Leadership Institute, 63

D

Danone, 48, 112
DaVita, 32, 35
Decathlon, 22
Dm-drogerie markt, 22
Dominant logic, 45

---

[1] Note: Page numbers followed by 'n' refer to notes.

© The Author(s) 2019
C. Rey et al. (eds.), *Purpose-driven Organizations*,
https://doi.org/10.1007/978-3-030-17674-7

E

Effectiveness, 60, 94, 106, 126
Emotions, 89, 105
Evaluation of purpose, 9

F

Facebook, 11, 114
Ferrer, 10, 89
Fortune magazine, 60
Four Seasons, 48
Fulfillment of purpose, 33, 36–38, 50, 51

G

Goal framing, 77
Google, 4, 11, 49, 50
Gore, 76

H

Habits, 38, 104, 105
Handelsbanken, 48
Harmonization, 8
Harvard Business School, 87
HCL Technologies, 23
Holacracy, 75, 84n2
HUF Portuguesa, 91

I

Identity, 14n22, 19, 20, 26n6, 26n7, 46, 64, 91, 98, 99, 102, 108, 110
IKEA, 49, 50
Implementation, 33, 36–39, 49, 78, 92, 99, 100, 116n19, 128n1
Insead, 35
Institutional logic, 46, 47, 50, 54n20, 54n22, 55n24, 55n25, 56n43
Integration, 36–39, 51, 81, 122
Integrity, 100, 101, 105, 129n18

Internalization, 32, 36–39, 87–94, 114, 116n31
ISS Facility Services, 8, 19, 35, 57

J

Jimenez Maña, 67, 83, 91
JJC, 91
Job, 6, 9, 14n22, 19, 23, 25, 40n26, 64, 78, 98, 129n3, 129n9
Johnson & Johnson, 50

K

KPMG, 21

L

La Fageda, 5
Leadership
  authentic leadership, 6
  purpose-driven leadership, 57–68
  servant leadership, 6
  shared leadership, 58, 59, 61–62, 68, 76, 91, 126
  transformational leadership, 19, 40n18, 60, 91
Legitimacy, 35, 50, 91, 107, 108, 115n4
Linear logic, 31–33
Logic of purpose, 3–12, 78, 84, 109

M

Management logic, 5, 6, 11–12, 13n11, 13n12, 13n14, 13n16
McDonalds, 31, 111
Medtronic, 8
Mercadona, 32
Mission, 4, 50, 51, 68n1, 76–84, 85n21, 85n22, 85n23, 85n24, 103, 104, 117n32, 117n45, 126, 128n1, 129n14
  effective mission, 33, 78–80, 100

Morning Star, 76, 80
Motivation, 18, 30–39, 48, 50, 59,
    60, 64, 78, 83, 85n20, 86n40,
    87, 91, 98–101, 103, 105,
    106, 109, 110, 112, 120, 126,
    127
  prosocial motivation, 38, 39, 48

N

NalonChem, 81
Narrative, 46, 87, 111, 113–115,
    117n38, 117n44
NASA, 18, 19, 25n1, 95n6
Nestlé, 113
New logic of purpose
  linear logic, 31–33
  oblique logic, 32
Nike, 114
Nokia, 35, 76
Novo Nordisk, 21

O

Objectives, 6, 9, 32, 36, 38, 39, 45, 49,
    54n23, 55n33, 77, 80, 81, 99,
    104, 108, 112, 115n9, 120, 124,
    125
Oblique logic, 32
Opportunity, 18, 45, 49, 93, 94, 105,
    109, 110
Organizational purpose, 4, 6–8, 13n17,
    34, 50, 60, 63, 66–68, 99,
    107–115, 121, 126

P

Patagonia, 76, 113, 114
Personal purpose, 4, 6–8, 10, 12,
    18–21, 23, 24, 26n14, 32,
    62–68, 83, 97–106, 127, 128
Profit maximization, 47–48

Purpose as action, 34–35
Purpose as knowledge, 33–34
Purpose as motivation, 35–36
Purpose development, 7, 19, 31–33,
    37, 49, 77, 102
Purpose fluidity, 20–23, 26n14
Purpose internalization, 37, 38,
    87–94
Purpose model canvas, 51–53
Purpose strength, 119–128
Purpose synergy, 20, 23–25

R

Reliability, 82
Repsol, 81

S

S&P, 107
Self-awareness, 103, 105
Self-knowledge, 102, 105
Self-management, 6, 8–9
Semillas Fitó, 80
Sephora, 48
Shared purpose, 25, 58, 62, 66, 68,
    84n13, 91, 109, 120–128
Singularity University, 49
Southwest Airlines, 109
Spotify, 80
Stakeholders, 4, 7, 33, 39, 50, 55n33,
    78, 81, 85n21, 85n23, 90,
    107–115, 128
Starbucks, 34, 114
Strategy, 7, 10, 36, 38, 44–53, 82, 83,
    90, 115, 117n41, 124

T

Tata, 4
TATA Group, 5, 32
TD Industries, 60

Team, 9, 10, 24, 36, 45, 62, 67, 78–83, 84n8, 87, 89, 121, 122, 126, 129n6
TED, 49
Telefónica, 8
Three dimensions of purpose, 30–39, 101
TOMS, 114
Two sides of purpose, 18–20
TZU CHI Hospital, 19

U
Unilever, 8, 67, 113
Unity, 6, 9–10, 18, 37, 68, 79, 108, 123, 128

V
Values, 6, 8–10, 13n11, 18, 22, 23, 30, 45–47, 49–52, 54n18, 58, 64, 89, 90, 93, 100–103, 105, 107–114, 126, 127
Vygon, 90

W
Walt Disney, 10, 31, 32, 113
Warby Parker, 34
Wikipedia, 83

Z
Zappos, 76, 114

CPSIA information can be obtained
at www.ICGtesting.com
Printed in the USA
LVHW081052300719
625731LV00026B/194/P